POSITIONING
YOUR CHILD *for*
Success

By

YVONNE POSEY GILCHRIST

Positioning Your Child for Success
by Yvonne Posey Gilchrist
FIRST EDITION

©2012 Yvonne Posey Gilchrist

ISBN #: 978-1-4675-4086-5

Editing / Packaging: Written Images, Detroit, Michigan
Cover Design: Erlene Taylor

For more information, to order additional copies, or to book Yvonne as a speaker, contact:

Complete Victory
YPG Consulting
35560 Grand River
Suite # 263
Farmington Hills, MI 48335-3123
Phone: 248.476.4817
Email: yvonne@positioningyourchild.com
Website: www.positioningyourchild.com

TABLE OF CONTENTS

SECTION THREE

College: It's Different Now

SECTION FOUR

The Portfolio—The Key to Your Child's Success from the Inside Out!

Acknowledgments

With God, all things are possible. This is most certainly true in my case because it is only by the amazing grace of God that I have come so far in such a brief period of time with so much to be thankful for.

Giving honor and glory to God Almighty and the Lord Jesus Christ, I am ever so thankful to the Holy Spirit for the depths of His goodness, His exceeding mercy and His amazing grace that has been bestowed upon me.

It is with great honor and deep humility that I express these words of acknowledgment. God gave me the vision for this book almost 3 years ago. I first shared that vision with my husband, Garlin Sr., and he has been my rock solid support ever since. Truly I have no words which fully express how much I love and thank the Lord for blessing me with just such a wonderful soul mate for life. Thank you Garlin for encouraging me to 'keep on keeping on' in the midst of great physical adversities and everyday ups and downs. Thank you for always seeing the finish line and always, always, always telling me that I would make it.

To my son, Garlin II: It has been my pleasure to share our journey in this book. I thank God for you and love you with all of my heart and soul. You have such a good spirit; you always listened and cooperated with us, and you trusted us to know what was best for you. My prayer is that the path that God allowed us to follow with you will indeed help other families be even more successful. I know that you will someday be a wonderful father to your children, continuing a very special legacy of success and faith in God for your family.

The second person that I shared that vision with is my dearest friend in the whole wide world, Sheila K. Scott. You encouraged me and pushed me and helped me find my balance when the scales tipped too far one way or the other. Your love as a sister, faithfulness as a friend and prayer partner will never, ever be forgotten. It is amazing to watch God move through those who love you. May you never stop interceding for me and my family. Thank you for such unconditional love.

To my editor, Diane P. Reeder: Thank you for incredible skill and anointing to walk with people like me. You make a difficult assignment seem easy and most certainly worth the journey. Thank you for a heart that has been tender towards me and for which I will be always be eternally grateful. Your efficiency and dedication humbles me. You are an amazing woman. You bear the load with such absolute grace and dignity. Please stay as sweet as you are forever. God has so much yet in store for you.

Acknowledgments

To my friend and sister in the ministry, Rev. Erlene Taylor: Thank you for your loyalty and friendship. Thank you for your unwavering willingness to help me do whatever needed to be done for this and so many other projects. Thank you for sticking ever so close by my side.

To my pastor, Rev. Dr. Nathan Johnson, First Lady Michael Michelle Johnson, the Tabernacle Missionary Baptist Church Family, and especially the New Hope Sunday School Class, for your ceaseless support of this project and for creating such a loving and nurturing Christian environment for Garlin II and his parents to grow and thrive within.

To Kenneth Hill, Detroit Area Pre-College Engineering Program (DAPCEP) Founder: Wow! Thank you for never giving up on your dream to create such a wonderful program for thousands of students and their parents. Thank you for caring about the success of children enough to never give up when times got tough. Thank you for being the wonderful caring man that you are. Please don't stop your great work preparing children to be successful!

To Suzanne Wasson, DAPCEP Program Administrator: Thank you for the outstanding work you have done with the DAPCEP K-3 Program Initiative. Your uncompromising spirit of excellence, and love for children and their families is exemplified in everything you do and manifests itself everywhere you go. Thank you for allowing me to grow under your loving and gracious care.

To Margaret Tucker, DAPCEP Program Administrator: Although you are retired now, the entire Gilchrist family will always love and appreciate you. Thank you for always thinking of Garlin II in such kind and unbelievable ways. Yours is a true friendship that will never be forgotten.

To Derrick E. Scott, Director of the Multicultural Engineering Programs Office at the University of Michigan College of Engineering: You literally made us part of the Michigan family! We are forever in your debt for opening doors of opportunity for our son. He can trace a big part of his success right back to you! Your important work with students speaks for itself and will never be forgotten.

To my sister, Bobbie Posey Milner: Thank you for enthusiastic support for this project. Your love has kept me uplifted and joyous about the possibilities God has laid out before us. Thank you for being the best sister ever!

To my mother, Mattie Posey: Thanks to you and Daddy (the late Dan Posey, Sr.) for taking such good and loving care of our infant son, Garlin. You set the standard. You showed me what a wonderful mother looks like. Then you went to the next level by showing all of us what a loving grandmother looked like. With the quiet grace of forged steel you met every challenge with amazing strength, dignity and love. I love you with all of my heart. Thank you for showing me how to be a good wife, mother and woman of God.

To our other parents, Doris and Isaac Gilchrist: Thanks, Mom and Dad, for all the love and support you gave our entire family. You gave of yourself without ceasing, pouring love and respect, dignity and honor, into our son without measure. You gave him a wonderful sense of heritage and

Acknowledgments

pride in who he is, and helped make him the man he ultimately came to be.

To the many parents, students, educators and other professionals that I have met along the way: Prayerfully our lives touched and I was able to positively affect you in some small way. You have impacted me on this journey as well. *Positioning Your Child for Success* is about the future because the future is where our hopes and dreams, prayers and faith in God reside.

May God bless your hearts today and always.

Yvonne

FIVE RULES TO POSITION YOUR CHILD FOR SUCCESS

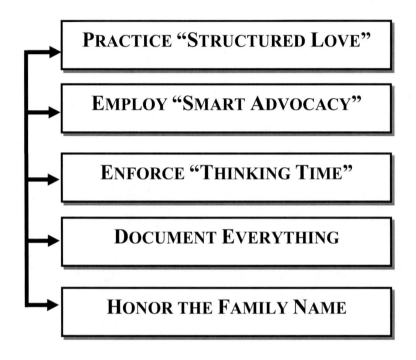

PRACTICE "STRUCTURED LOVE"

EMPLOY "SMART ADVOCACY"

ENFORCE "THINKING TIME"

DOCUMENT EVERYTHING

HONOR THE FAMILY NAME

Want to know more? Keep reading…

Introduction

Just imagine…

Robert is a successful 28-year-old with a dual undergraduate degree in Computer Engineering and Computer Science Engineering. He is headed down a promising career path. He was an excellent student in high school, and was accepted at several promising colleges. In fact, he was offered more than a half-million dollars in scholarship money. His success continued even after he walked across the stage with his college degree; companies rushed to make attractive offers and he had many, many options.

Robert's mother, Rachel, knows exactly why her son was so successful.

Rachel has a friend, Barbara, whose son has not had the same successes. Barbara loves her son very much. She's spent what she believes is quality time with him. She was diligent in meeting with his teachers, helping him with his homework, and making sure he was exposed to extracurricular activities. However, Barbara's son, William, dropped out of college and has floundered ever since. She's not sure what to do now, and so she asked her friend.

"Rachel, what did you do that was different from me?"

Rachel is gentle but firm. "Barbara," she says, "there are a couple of ways to 'love' your child. You can watch them like a hawk—do their homework, complain constantly to their teachers, over-commit them to the activities you wish you had engaged in as a teenager...and you'll end up with one of two outcomes: a floundering child who doesn't know what to do, or a successful but neurotic child who is incapable of taking personal responsibility and 'owning' their own success."

"The other way," she explained further, "is the way my husband Bob and I have done it. You can pay attention to who your child really is. That takes real work. You have to understand the gifts, talents, interests and abilities that the Lord has placed on the inside of your child. You encourage them, and ensure that they have every opportunity to fully explore those abilities and interests. As you give them opportunities and the freedom to explore, you'll find that most will discover and pursue their passion. They will ultimately become successful because they are able to do what they love, and they have learned how to think on their own and how to make good positive decisions for themselves. You are, in essence, your child's facilitator—not their dictator or controller. Your job is to help them discover their true purpose. It is in discovering that purpose that real joy in life happens, and that is ultimately what we want for our children."

Introduction

"But I helped William with his homework!" protested Barbara. "I all but did it myself. I met with his teachers, I put him in everything...basketball, soccer, Great Books classes...I got so tired I felt like I was the student!"

Rachel looked at her friend. She didn't want to say the obvious.

"Instead of doing his homework, maybe you should have done your homework."

"What's that?" asked Barbara.

"The hard work of learning your child as a unique, individual person, and crafting a plan that is consistent with who he is instead of who you want him to be," Rachel answered. "None of this happens by osmosis...it's not going to just come to you. I don't care how brilliant your child is; success is where <u>preparation</u> meets <u>opportunity</u>."

She immediately felt bad giving Barbara that hindsight advice. "There's still time," she said as she sought to comfort her friend.

~

This is a story that I have seen repeated and repeated too many times. It's a fictional story, but one that comes from a mix of real-life stories that I have heard in more than 20 years of speaking to students and parents about preparing their children for success.

Rachel's story is essentially my story. My name is Yvonne Posey Gilchrist, and my son, Garlin Dorell Gilchrist

II (Garlin), 28, works as the Director of New Media for The Center for Community Change in Washington, D.C. He graduated from a local suburban Detroit high school with a 3.9 grade point average (GPA). After being named "High School Male Student of the Year" by the National Society of Black Engineers (NSBE), and applying to several colleges and universities, he received more than $750,000 (that's seven-hundred-fifty *thousand* dollars) in scholarships, and ultimately chose the University of Michigan, where he received enough scholarships to pay for college tuition, room and board, books, fees, and everything else he could possibly need. Garlin later graduated with dual degrees in Computer Engineering and Computer Science Engineering. He graduated with a 3.4 GPA, and his first job was with one of the premier companies in the world, Microsoft Corporation. He is now married to a wonderful young woman, and my husband and I couldn't be more proud!

How did it happen? My husband and I agree on this short answer: *"Not by accident."*

The investment we made in our child was not solely an investment of money. We deliberately positioned him for success by following a concept you will see repeated many times in this book: *Structured Love.*

We'll talk later about Garlin's early years. For now, I'll just tell you about how our son got involved in the field of engineering.

Introduction

In 1992, I was sitting under the hair dryer at my local beauty shop. (It helps sometimes to be outgoing.) I was chatting, as best I could with the dryer noise in my ears, with a lady who was telling me about her middle-school-aged son who had just come back from spending four weeks on the University of Michigan campus in a program called the "Summer Engineering Academy." I put the dryer up so I could hear better.

"What did you say?" I asked her.

I drilled her for the entire time I was at the beauty shop. "What is DAPCEP? What does it stand for?" She told me that it stood for the Detroit Area Pre-College Engineering Program. "You mean to tell me these kids get to go to college for free?!" I said, shocked. "Actually, yes," the lady told me patiently. She was really friendly.

I needed to hear about this because, at the time, my son was in the fifth grade. The woman I spoke to did not know what the age range was, so I called the DAPCEP office early that following Monday morning to inquire about enrolling my son.

"Lady, you are a year early," said the individual who answered the phone.

Now this is what I mean by doing your homework. I didn't make a note to myself to call them in a year.

"What can I do?" I asked. "I want to find out more about this DAPCEP program."

"We have a Parent Advisory Committee that's kind of like the PTA," the person on the telephone replied.

Right then and there, I decided to join the DAPCEP Parent Advisory Committee (PAC). I figured that if I could find out more about DAPCEP from the parents, I would gain really good insight into the program from their unique perspective. Plus, it was something I could do NOW, a year ahead of time, to gain hands-on knowledge prior to my son enrolling in the program.

I ended up working with those parents and DAPCEP for the next eight years. I remained a member of the PAC until Garlin graduated from high school. During that time, I joined and/or chaired several committees, with a keen focus on the Education Committee. It was on that committee that I learned the "college game." We organized college fairs, hosted career days, and I had a unique opportunity to connect with key college contacts. I attribute my work on that Committee to our family's ability to secure those scholarships for Garlin in abundance. I remain involved in DAPCEP's critical outreach programs for urban students today, because I am eternally grateful for the role that DAPCEP and the University of Michigan played in positioning our son for success.

Whenever I speak at events for parents, I find parents asking me the same basic question: *"How do you raise a successful child?"* The more I talk to them, the more I realize that this is the most important work we do as parents.

Introduction

I would have to say that probably the most important word I would use for the nature of parental involvement is **engagement.**

My husband Garlin Sr. (I'll refer to him as Garlin Sr. and to our son simply as Garlin) and I believe in strong parental involvement. Garlin had a mother and father who were always involved in his endeavors. As a parent advocate, I always stressed that you have to be connected in order to ensure your child's success. I call it, "Position Your Child for Success."

Your child will not become successful by osmosis; while you are their most important role model, your child won't just automatically follow his or her own path to purpose without your systematic, planned, deliberate, thoughtful, and in our case, prayerful involvement.

If you do nothing and your child does nothing, the end product you achieve will certainly be nothing or somewhere close to that. We have to *steer* our children in the right direction, and help them stay on track. The better the partnership between you and your child, the greater his or her chances for success.

You may be familiar with the Bible verse found in Proverbs 22:6 that says, "Raise up a child in the way he should go, and when he is old he will not depart from it." For years many of us learned that verse meant simply, "Raise them right." Well, that isn't the whole story. A more complete translation goes something like this: "Raise up a child according to the way he should go *and in keeping with his individual gift or bent...*" In other words, look at the way they're made—the interests they have, their gifts, their talents, their psychological makeup. As parents, God gives us insight into who our children are. We have a singular opportunity to talk to them, hear what's on their mind and in their heart, and push them into those directions that we feel they are capable of exploring at just the right moments in time. I believe that we should expose our children to a variety of different experiences so that they get a "grand look," so to speak, at the rich possibilities that life offers. This increases their self-awareness, and helps them get to know themselves better—their likes and dislikes, their strengths and weaknesses. It also teaches them how to positively explore options and how to make critical judgments or decisions about what works and what does not work for them. The point here is for parents to facilitate these experiences so that the child has an opportunity to think critically about what is going on and to make choices.

Do you remember the story of Jesus turning the water into wine? Do you remember who prompted Him to do that?

Mary and her son, Jesus, were at a wedding in the village of Cana. The hosts had run out of wine. Mary knew who her son was and what He had been called to do. (See John 2:1-11)

"They have run out of wine," she told Him. Her expectation was for Jesus to solve the problem.

Jesus was human, wasn't He? He wasn't exactly motivated to do what His mother expected Him to do at that particular moment in time. Look at how He answered His mother:

"What does your concern have to do with Me? My hour has not yet come." (NKJV) or "That's not our problem, my time has not yet come." (NLT)

Mary was undaunted in her confidence that her son could solve this problem. She refused to give up, ignoring his seeming lack of motivation. She looked to the servants of the house. "Whatever He tells you to do, do it," she instructed them. She had complete confidence that He could solve this problem, even though he had not yet demonstrated any interest in responding.

Jesus made a decision to respond. "Fill the jars with water," He directed the servants.

The results were impressive. It turned out that Jesus miraculously changed the water in those jars into fine wine. One high level official attending the wedding as a guest lauded the master of the house. "Everyone starts these events with the best wine," he exclaimed, "but you have saved the best for last!"

Jesus's mother knew her son was ready. She knew that He was put on earth to do a significant work. She was not sure exactly how this would happen, but she had complete confidence in Him to solve that particular problem on that particular day.

I firmly believe that God gives parents insight into their children's gifts and talents, even into the timing of those gifts or talents. Sometimes our kids don't see it; but it is our job to nurture them, to assist, to encourage, and to lead them into their giftings so that they, and the whole world, can benefit. Sometimes, when we least expect it, we can move our children to make miracles - in their sight and ours!

~

I knew that Garlin was very good in math and science. That's why this particular program, DAPCEP, was of such significant interest to me. And I knew this not just because the engineering field presented a promising future career choice. If Garlin had had a particular "bent" for art, for example, my beauty shop encounter may have not been as significant. I would have been looking for opportunities for him to explore his artistic gifts. But this was engineering, science, technology and math, and I knew my son had talent in these areas. Plus, I knew that he needed math and science in college, regardless of his career aspirations. At the end of the day, I knew that if he was well-prepared, he'd be able to land that all-important, yet sometimes elusive, "good" job!

This is not the first book on child-rearing and child-raising, and it certainly won't be the last. But it is one of the first books to actually take you, step-by-step, age-by-age, grade-by-grade, through a proven process that will put your child in a position to be successful.

That's all we can ask or do, isn't it? To give our children the tools and direction they need to be ready for success when it presents itself. And to make sure that it does indeed present itself.

This book is meant to be used as a guide. Hopefully, your child is about two or three years old right now; but if not, know that it's never too late!

Introduction

Before you get immersed in your plans and structure, there is one very important thing that I will state right up front: *enjoy your child*. Delight in him or her. They are God's reward, and they are precious. But in your enthusiasm, delight and joy, make sure that your love and care are accompanied by a plan for success.

This book will show you how to do just that.

We'll talk first about *the power of words* in your child's life—specifically, your words. They're more powerful than you think. We'll move to the concept of *structured love* and how that plays out on a day-to-day basis. We'll take you through a step-by-step description of what you as a parent should be doing to maximize your child's development with age-appropriate strategies and activities. We'll talk about the critical senior year, and focus on the dual searches for colleges and scholarships.

Next, we'll talk about how to let your child "go" once they leave for college. Well, not exactly let them *go*, but loosen the strings and move from closely guarding parent to wise and trusted advisor.

Finally, we'll talk about developing your child's portfolio. Portfolios are not just for artists; they are ways to document and personalize your child's gifts, talents, abilities and successes for those who make decisions about academic programs, top schools, scholarships, awards, and jobs. The portfolio is the tool that can put your child in the most competitive position possible, and actually helps boost their confidence as they see their portfolio grow from kindergarten through college.

Essentially, this book is about preparing and promoting—the twin strategies that ensure that your child is ready, and that others know about it.

SECTION ONE

Love In Action

CHAPTER 1

Word! The Power of What You Say to Your Child

I n this chapter, we're going to talk about the power of your words. Words are the first things your child hears from you, and what you say at every stage is going to impact their success more powerfully than just about anything else you or anyone else will do for them.

When I was a child, I heard over and over the old saying, "Sticks and stones may break my bones, but words will never hurt me." I am here today to tell you that is absolutely untrue. Words are powerful; they can murder a person's soul or spirit just as completely as a gun or knife. The damage of words can linger in the heart and mind for years beyond the date they were actually spoken. Words can tear down, burn down, break down, or wear down the weary soul. Proverbs

18:21 reads, "Words kill, words give life, they're either poison or fruit—you choose." (The Message)

I can remember a time when I was about ten years old. I joined my church's youth choir. There was a mean bully of a girl in the choir, and one day she said to me, "You can't sing. You're not on beat. You sound horrible." Her words humiliated me, and worse yet, humiliated me in front of all my peers.

I only stayed in that choir a couple of weeks, and I've never been to one since. Ironically, I love to sing and I sing all the time. But I remembered those words for a very long period of time, and they hurt. It took quite some time for me to understand that her words did not apply to me, and for me to undo the damage that was done. I was so pleased with myself when I came to realize that my joy of singing and my ability to sing came from the Lord. It was at that point that I sang and sang with exceeding joy and, most importantly to me, great personal satisfaction and confidence.

Words do matter.

Parents, please, if you don't get anything else out of this book, get this: your words DO matter and they are powerful. I trust that you already know that, but sometimes we forget.

Too often, the root of the 'harmful words' problem is not the child, but animosity toward the other parent. "You're worthless, just like your Daddy." "You're nothing, just like your Mama." We beat our children down with animosity not even meant for them, but when heard often enough, those negative or mean-spirited messages meant for an estranged or former spouse or partner can cause nearly irreparable damage to our children.

We are a family of faith in God, and we stood on that faith daily, trusting the Lord to help our family in every way and to keep our son safe and secure each day.

When my child was about twelve years old, I would wake up early every weekday morning and go into his bedroom. I would speak words of blessing over my child such as, "Garlin, your mother and dad love you very much. Jesus loves you even more. He will command His blessings to come upon you and to overtake you, when you obey His voice. You will be blessed everywhere you go. You will be blessed when you come in and when you go out. You will be blessed in your body and blessed in the work that you do. All that you put your hand and heart to perform you will be able to do. You are the head and not the tail. You are a leader and not a follower. You are above and not beneath. You are a child of God and wherever the soles of your feet walk, it's holy ground. You will be kept safe. Your school will be safe, and I pray that you will have favor that surrounds you like a shield, favor with the students and favor with your teachers. I pray that your memory will be blessed by God and that your mind will be clear and sharp to do exceedingly abundantly well in all of your school work and activities."

Most of the time, he knew I was there. He wouldn't always wake up fully, but he would smile.

If Garlin had a test, or a game, or any other challenge, we'd pray over it. I made sure that our ministering angels were on assignment 24/7!

Garlin was not left out of this prayer process. We taught him how to cover himself in the Lord. We taught him that it was important for him to trust the Lord each day for himself, as well as for others. I had him read a chapter from the Book of Proverbs each day. Proverbs, considered one of the Bible's "Wisdom Books," happens to have 31 chapters— one for each day of the month. On the first day of the month, I would have him read Proverbs 1, on the second day Proverbs 2, etc.

You might ask yourself why I did all of this each morning. The answer is quite simple: Love. If I didn't speak words of protection, provision, success and blessings over my child, who else was going to do it? I certainly couldn't— shouldn't—expect his teachers or some other authority figure in his life to do what I wasn't willing to do myself. NO! He was my son, the gift that God gave my husband and I. Along with that gift came a tremendous responsibility to raise him up in the fear and admonition of the Lord. I was accountable and I did not take that accountability lightly. Faith must be practiced. It must be put to the test. I trusted the Lord to help my child, to protect my child, and to mold and shape him into the person he was meant to be. I wanted Garlin to see and know that he was covered in God.

The world comes to our children with so many challenges to their humanity. It may be in the form of their teachers, their peers, law enforcement...even family members sometimes! As parents, it is our job to do the very

4

best that we can to send them out into the world prepared and fortified against any harmful worldly onslaughts.

> *"Words kill, words give life; they're either poison or fruit—you choose."*

~Proverbs 18:21 (The Message)

But despite our best intentions, hurtful words do indeed slip out. In those hopefully rare instances, we must learn to ask our children's forgiveness. Tell them something like this:

"CHILD'S NAME, I'm so sorry. You know, you didn't come with an instruction manual and sometimes I get frustrated. I took that frustration out on you, and you don't deserve it. Please forgive me."

Come in the right spirit, and they will forgive you. Show forgiveness yourself when they make mistakes, and they'll be sure to show it back.

Building Up, Not Tearing Down

You can't be too generous with your child in praising their accomplishments. When they go out to school, you can tell them:

"You look nice today."

"Have a good day."

"Have a blessed day."

(When they're younger) *"Didn't you do a good job tying your shoes? Wow!"*

5

POSITIONING YOUR CHILD FOR SUCCESS

We're not talking about unearned, ingratiating praise. Phrases like, *"You are so great!"* can be meaningless if not connected to some particular accomplishment. In other words, don't make up praise. Find something your child has done well, and be very specific in your "praise-ology." Even if they only did half of what they were supposed to do, praise that half FIRST before you challenge them to complete the other half as well. *"I see you made up the bed. Good job. Now, let's finish cleaning the floor just like you did your bed."*

Our children get enough verbal "beat-downs." As parents, we must not add to that.

YOUR HOMEWORK

In the chart below, indicate the harmful things you say to your child, and replace those harmful sayings with words and phrases designed to encourage and strengthen your child.

Harmful Words	Constructive Words

"Encourage each other every day while you have the opportunity..."

~Hebrews 3:13a (God's Word)

6

CHAPTER 2

Structured Love

"Everybody in this house has a job."

We made going to work serious business, something that every member of the Gilchrist family had to do. Dad had a job. Mom had a job. Garlin had a job as well. That first job was to go to Grandma's house and have her babysit him.

As he got older, his job changed. He went to pre-school. Garlin took his job seriously. "I'm going to work," he would tell us as we strapped him into his car seat. By the time he was three, he had a spoon to dig the weeds out of the cracks in the sidewalk while his dad mowed the lawn.

When Garlin was four, his dad gave him a little shovel. It was snowing, and he was to help his dad shovel the snow. One day, it was so cold, I called him back into the house for some hot chocolate to warm him up. When Garlin Sr. noticed that Garlin was missing and had gone back inside of the house, he came inside and asked me, "What are you doing?"

"He was shivering so," was my reply. I couldn't stand to see my baby out there in the cold.

"A man has to finish his work," said Garlin Sr. "I'm cold too but there is still work to be done. We will both come back when the job is finished." He put Garlin back into his snowsuit, gave him back his little shovel and marched my baby back outside into the shivering cold to finish the job.

I learned something very important that day. I could be Garlin's mother, but I could never be his father. It takes a man to do that. It takes a man to teach a man to become a man. As Garlin Sr. and I discussed the matter in detail later that evening, I realized that I interfered where I should not have. The very characteristics that I admired in my husband—a hard worker, steadfastness, stick-to-it-ness, not a quitter—were qualities that had to be developed in the young man we were raising. If I allowed or even worse encouraged my son to stop working just because he was a little cold, or a little tired, or just plain didn't feel like doing the job, then what kind of man would I be raising? One that started jobs but never finished them? How many women today are married to these kinds of men and are not happy about it? If I wanted my child to stay with a matter until the end, then that characteristic had to be nurtured when he was small and reinforced constantly all the way through manhood. I truly thank the Lord that my husband had the foresight to know that and turned the situation around to effect a worthy lesson for both me and my young son.

If not his father, it can be a grandfather, an uncle, an older brother, or even a family friend or teacher.

By the time he was in first grade, Garlin clearly understood that his job was to learn, to get a good education.

How Much is Too Much?

There is a limit to how tough we should be on our children at various stages of their development. We may insist that our four-year-old shovel a certain, limited amount of snow. When they get older, we will insist that they finish their homework before allowing them to play outside. But there is always the risk of going too far. Making the four-year-old stay out until they become dangerously cold would be a mistake. Insisting that our eight-year-old focus on academics to the neglect of healthy social interaction and play would also be inappropriate. These are examples of toughness going too far.

The answer to this question rests in establishing age-appropriate structures for your child as soon as possible. This is very important, because it establishes the boundaries for what to do and when to do it. Obviously, Garlin would not have been able to shovel snow before he could walk. Obviously, at four years old he couldn't shovel the entire driveway. But little baby steps, like shoveling our small front porch, were specifically designed to prepare him for those larger feats. This parameter was established to reinforce the idea that we were a family and in a family there was ALWAYS work to be done, and that he would always have a share of that work to do.

Child-rearing is essentially a series of ever-expanding boundaries. After all, at birth, they have no boundaries, and the parent must work really hard in the beginning to "tighten the net" by meeting their immediate needs for food, clothing, shelter, and boundless affection. Once that infant figures out that he or she won't perish, we begin to construct a series of basic boundaries. We now sleep at night. We now eat at certain hours during the day. We now play at certain other times. We progress into helping them learn things. They learn to walk. They learn to talk. They learn there is much to explore, and our very first job in this is to make sure they don't harm themselves in all of their exploration. Touch this, not that. Eat this, not that. Go here, not there. Play in the family room, but not in the street.

When Garlin was about three years old, Garlin Sr. and I put a big toy chest in the family room. "You can play with any toy in this chest that you wish, but when it is time to clean up you will have to put that toy back into the toy chest," we told him. Guess what? Our little boy had a problem with this at first. But we were willing to wait all day if that's what it took to teach him this clean-up after yourself lesson. Garlin quickly learned which lines to cross and which not to cross, and the consequences for crossing those lines.

Children without boundaries are destined to live out-of-control lives. Sure, they can physically drive up to the maximum number on their car's speedometer. But in short order, they'll run into a wall, or another car, or a police officer that will stop them, and end up hurt, in jail or dead. Parents who do not teach their children boundaries will subject them to the risk of tragic consequences.

> *"Don't fail to correct your children. You won't kill them by being firm."*
> ~Proverbs 23:13 (CEV)

Structured love helps a child understand where they fit. It proves to them that they belong to a family, and that they are loved.

The worst thing you can say to a child is, "I don't care. Do whatever you want to do. I don't care about the choices you make. I don't care about the friends you hang around with. I don't care what you do or who you do it with." Setting no boundaries brings pain, not pleasure, to a child's life. Setting age-appropriate boundaries for your children lets them know that you care about their physical, emotional, psychological, and spiritual well-being. It shows them, even better than telling them, that they matter very, very much to you.

Balancing Work and Play

Garlin is a big man now, standing at a cool 6'8". As soon as he got out of the crib, his dad placed a basketball in his hands. My husband thought they both would be going to the NBA *and* the NFL together! With our son's academic, church, and extracurricular activities, our family had to do a

11

dance of sorts - maintaining the very delicate balance between academics and athletics, church, family and community service. I cannot count how many times I stared coaches in the face and said, "We'll be there after DAPCEP," which took up six weeks in the fall, six weeks in the spring, and four weeks in the summer, leaving 36 weeks to get all the rest done.

Even though we emphasized academics, we made time for Garlin's other interests as well—in an engaged and enthusiastic way. I was the super athletic mom at the concession stand, and the sports fund raising mom extraordinaire. We were just as excited about Garlin's sports prowess (the things HE was excited about) as we were about his academic prowess (the things WE were excited about). Children appreciate that kind of balanced enthusiasm and interest, and with that parental enthusiasm they know that their parents care genuinely about who they really are and what they are actually doing.

As parents we need to support our children in *everything* they do. I couldn't support Garlin s educational activities and then shun the other things he wanted to be a part of, so I was just as enthusiastic about all the other "stuff" that he was doing as I was about his educational endeavors.

We had a very important family rule. To be able to do those "other" things like sports, Garlin had to handle his business. That "business" for him represented his academic responsibilities, as well as his responsibilities around the house, within the family, at church, and at school.

Structured love literally *brainwashes* children into thinking that they are competent and full of worth. When you give them outlets for their talents and interests, provide them with meaningful work, and support their aspirations, dreams and projects, they come to believe that they are valuable human beings with something significant to offer the world.

And guess what? They are absolutely right.

YOUR HOMEWORK

Name five things that you are currently doing that demonstrate "structured" love.

1. _____

2. _____

3. _____

4. _____

5. _____

Name five things you can do that you are *not* currently doing that will demonstrate "structured" love.

1. _____

2. _____

3. _____

4. _____

5. _____

POSITIONING YOUR CHILD FOR SUCCESS

Name five activities you can give to your child to introduce the concept of work.

1. _____

2. _____

3. _____

4. _____

5. _____

"So we rebuilt the wall, which was rebuilt to about half of its [original] height. The people worked with determination.

~Nehemiah 4:6 (God's Word)

CHAPTER 3

Structured Love in Action— The Pre-School Years

I always felt that Garlin was a special gift to me. What mother, what parent, doesn't feel that way? And so, I felt an awesome responsibility to do right by this gift—to honor what God gave me. Unquestionably, God gives you gifts and talents, but He also expects you to be accountable. So, Garlin Sr. and I had a responsibility on a proactive basis to create a Godly home, and to nurture and discipline our son.

Now I must admit, Garlin was the BEST baby in the whole wide world; he had the brightest smile, he was even-tempered, and had a wonderful spirit. We surrounded him with love, which made him open to interacting positively with others, even non-family members. He never experienced the concept of "not belonging."

But NOBODY knew that Garlin was an only child; unless they asked him how many sisters or brothers he had. When anyone, family or not, described our son, they would never use the word "spoiled."

Why? Because we raised him deliberately, with a philosophy I referred to earlier as "Structured Love."

I never moved a breakable trinket or had to "childproof" our home; I just told Garlin what was in-bounds and what was out-of-bounds. "You have complete freedom in the family room," I would tell him in words he could understand, "but the living room coffee table is out-of-bounds."

There's immense freedom in providing appropriate information to your child. When children know what's what, what gets them into trouble and what keeps them out of it, they're much more comfortable and much happier. That's "Structured Love." If you tell them to do whatever they want, that concept is too large. That's "Unstructured Love," and it allows for too many choices at one time. Children won't know what to choose, or what to do. This confuses children and often times leads to that dreaded phrase, "I'm bored."

You can never start "structure" too early. You may begin soon after birth.

Establish Bedtime

As soon as possible, establish a specific bedtime hour. Of course, during the first few months you'll be getting up for nighttime feedings and diaper changes, but after that you

16

begin to train your child to go to bed according to a schedule. Maybe that bedtime is 7:00 or 8:00 p.m.; an infant, after all, needs about 18 hours of sleep per day. If they cry, make sure that they have been well-fed, that they are dry, that there is nothing sticking or poking them, that they are not sick or running a fever, and that they are comfortable. If everything checks out, repeat this mantra to yourself to avoid the inevitable guilt feelings you experience as a new, loving parent:

"Tears never killed anybody. Tears never killed anybody. Tears never killed anybody."

Say it three times, and make yourself wait to go into your baby's room early the next morning, as long as you have first checked to make sure they are alright; they will get over it!

Avoid the "Helicopter Syndrome"

You've heard the phrase "Helicopter Moms," haven't you? Those are mothers who tend to hover over their children, taking in their every breath and, in the process, taking the breath out of their children as well. This often happens as the child moves into school age; the mother will constantly ask what they're doing, they won't let the child out of their sight.

This "helicopter" syndrome typically begins at birth, and it's not healthy. We live in an age where children are extremely self-centered; they expect accolades for doing what previous generations' parents minimally expected their children to do: make up their beds, do chores, get good grades. I suggest that part of the reason for this is that we are overly consumed with our children.

Think about previous generations. Did they feel they had to entertain their children 24/7? Of course not! They physically could not, because there was the cooking, the cleaning, the washing, drying and sewing of clothes, the hunting for food, and often times other children to attend to—all without today's modern conveniences. There was no time!

So guess what? The child had to entertain him- or herself. What a concept— that a child could actually be satisfied with his or her own company! Now, that's a way to build self-esteem that doesn't require you to stand around clapping for your child every time they do something, significant or not.

Am I saying to ignore your child? Of course not. I'm just cautioning you not to be overly consumed with your child. When you're busy, they should be busy, and not busy watching TV but busy exploring themselves and their world. You should not allow your child to interrupt the activities that you must engage in as a parent to keep your household running. The world has so many artificial stimulations; what about encouraging our children to be comfortable when absolutely NOTHING is going on—no TV or radio or cell phones or video games or iPods, iPads, mp3 players or Wii's—just flowers growing or birds singing or dogs barking?

I am a strong believer in "forced nothing."

With outside, artificial "noise" going on all the time, the child gets a very dangerous message. They come to believe that the world is responsible for stimulating and entertaining them. Why is that dangerous? It is because the world's stimulation and entertainment is not always wholesome or life-affirming. Far better for the child to get the message that they can look inside themselves for strength, for comfort, and even for stimulation—by their own thoughts, reflections and discoveries.

In fact, I worked to instill reflection even during Garlin's nap time. Like most children, he resisted naps and would try talking me into expanding his waking time. So I had a great "trick:" At home, Garlin's bed always faced a window. Therefore I told him to look out of the window. "See the beauty of nature all around you," I told him, "and talk to God."

"God loves you and always wants to talk to you and hear what you have to say," I told him. (After all, it was—and is still—true) "Lie down and talk to the Lord. Tell Him whatever you want to tell Him. Then listen and hear what He has to say. When you get up, tell me what God said to you."

He rarely stayed awake more than five minutes once he was down. That helped me a LOT. But the greatest benefit was that he learned how to talk to, and listen for, God's voice.

Remember, you will not always be there.

Look for Your Child's Special Qualities

Even at the age of two and three, I was on the lookout for Garlin's talents and gifts. One day when he was three years old, we noticed how much he was flipping and tumbling, so I decided to enroll him in gymnastics school to help him flip correctly. Again, we were building in structure—not in a rigid, controlling way, but in a way that honored and nurtured him in the area of his natural giftedness. That was the beginning of organized play.

Then, we joined the YMCA and enrolled in a class for mom and tot swimming. I didn't even know how to swim, but I got in the water anyway. Lucky for me it was only four feet deep. I have a deathly fear of water, but I didn't want Garlin to have the same inhibitions. I did manage to learn to float pretty well. At the "Y", I saw other courses—art, basketball, tennis, karate—so I just started enrolling Garlin in the different classes as they appeared in the catalog. They issued a catalog every six weeks, and I made sure we were on the mailing list.

This brings me to another important point. You have to pay attention to the kind of child you have. Long before Garlin started pre-school, we found that he needed an outlet for physical activity. Garlin loved to run and jump and play; he almost never stopped moving!

As parents, we should encourage physical play and activity. There is an increasing problem of obesity and near-obesity among children, and there is almost no excuse for that. You don't have to force a child into highly physical, competitive sports if they don't want to be there. They might be happier in less competitive activities such as dance, swimming or gymnastics. The point here is to find some type of physical outlet for your child.

The important take-away here? Know Your Child.

The Importance of Multiple Environments

I hear a lot from parents who complain about how their parents interact with their grandchildren. The most frequent complaint is that, "Mom/Dad just spoils them so; when Johnny/Ruthie comes back they're a mess, and I have to re-train them all over again."

I have a free tip for you. It comes from America's father, Bill Cosby. He says that grandparents spoil their grandchildren because "they're trying to get into heaven now."

My father switched his shift to work midnights just so he could see Garlin in the mornings. My aunt would babysit him while my mother cooked. I bought an extra high chair for my parents' house, but my mother turned it away. "We don't need that high chair. We hold our babies around here!" Of course, at home Garlin Sr. and I couldn't possibly hold him all the time, but it was okay. He got 24/7 nurturing love at the home where I had been mothered and fathered. It was like Grand Central Station over at the grandparents— everybody talking at once, loads of visitors and lots of excitement—just like when I was growing up. That environment didn't hurt me and it didn't hurt our son. Quite the contrary, he thrived.

We trusted my parents. They could do whatever they wanted to do with our child. They'd raised us, and had done a pretty good job. I didn't mind that each of his extended family members had their own ways of helping to raise him.

We trusted Garlin Sr.'s parents too, of course. Their home was much more serene, so when Garlin went there he had a completely different experience. There, he was calm and quiet, and could probably hear himself think a little bit better than when he was at my parent's house.

But wherever he was, whatever the style of the environment, certain things were constant. Garlin was loved, and he was safe, and he was cared for. It was a very special time for him.

We did have to help our son get used to the different caregiving environments. We let Garlin know that the rules were different at our home. No carrying him on my hip around the clock; no rich soul food at six months like my mother fed him; and later, and no getting around the set nap time.

What's the lesson here? Forget about trying to make uniform environments for every place your child goes. After all, they're going to have to adjust to multiple environments when they go to school. They'll have easy teachers, hard teachers, nice ones, mean ones, and indifferent ones. Why not let them get used to multiple environments and different kinds of caregiving early, before they even get to school? As long as the environment is safe and loving, your child should be alright. You must learn to embrace the rich, diverse relationships that these multiple interactions and environments afford for your child.

Minimize the "Baby Talk"

It's okay to coo, ooh and aah, but TALK, really talk, to your child as much as possible. Language is the gateway to concepts and ideas. Start with short sentences and words, then move to longer, more complex sentences. And read, read, read to your child. I started reading to Garlin while he was in the womb. They really do hear your voice and studies suggest that babies who are spoken to in the womb actually pay more attention to the voice of the one who spoke.

Your child will speak enough "baby talk" by themselves. They don't need you to help them do that. What they need from you is language development.

Staying Inside the Lines

"Play is the work of the child."

~Maria Montessori

After experiencing these great, loving multiple environments of his grandparents, Garlin was blessed to attend a fantastic pre-school that I found for him when he was four years old. In his early years, he had interacted primarily with adults, and I was looking to help him begin socializing with other children.

Garlin was ready. He'd had the early educational benefit of my sister, who was a first-grade teacher extraordinaire and applied her excellent teaching skills to him, helping him to sound out words before he even started school. He ended up with a wonderful pre-school teacher and participated in a great program. It required that parents spend at least a couple of hours one day per week in the classroom with their child. His dad and I were so impressed that we each insisted on spending one day per week! The environment was nurturing; they made learning fun and reinforced the values we were trying to instill in Garlin. We also learned about some of the best ways to teach young children. In fact, this was our foray into parental involvement in education, and provided an impetus for us to continue a similarly intense involvement throughout his entire educational life. He went to Kindergarten at this location as well.

The first song Garlin learned in pre-school was "Color the circle purple, color the circle purple, color the circle purple, and stay inside the lines." Garlin had never colored between the lines before, but he did once he learned that song. When the teacher wanted him to sit in a certain chair, she would say, "Sit in the BLUE chair," or, "Sit in the ORANGE chair." When she directed the children to bring something, it was, "Please bring the GREEN placemat." This was a great way to learn colors, and we continued the practice at the dinner table. Every vegetable and fruit had a color, and we built upon his pre-school experience by identifying carrots as orange and bananas as yellow—every time.

This was an important time for yet another reason as well. It was here that I came to recognize my own deficits. I was clearly *not* the person to be teaching her own kid at this level. Qualified professionals can make all the difference in the world. I had spent years trying to teach Garlin to 'stay inside the coloring book lines,' and here this teaching professional was able to accomplish that goal in just one day!

Parents, be open to what YOU can learn about teaching your children from their teachers. Shame on us if we fail to respect the true professional educators that help our children fly! If you expose your children to skilled professionals who have a loving, nurturing spirit, they can learn anything.

The Work-Play Balance

As I mentioned earlier, Garlin Sr. provided the "work" in the work-play balance for Garlin. I've already shared with you the snow shoveling story, where I was so tempted to stop my "mean" husband from making my little baby shovel the snow in the cold, and he reassured me that our baby wouldn't suffer from frostbite, or remember this as a traumatic life experience. Dad was just showing him, gradually and age-appropriately, how to grow into responsible manhood.

I have another, similar story. One day, when Garlin was about four years old, my husband gave him a spoon and told him to come outside. "What's the spoon for?" I wondered. I soon found out.

"Your job is to dig the weeds out of the cracks in the driveway," Garlin Sr. explained to Garlin. You should have seen our small son as he carefully grasped the small spoon and proudly began digging into the cracks. It was worth it just to see the smile on his face as he earnestly pulled out the weeds and placed them in a pile on the sidewalk, then took them to the trash for disposal. Garlin started our son working early in life, before he knew enough to question, and when "helping Daddy" was still an exciting and attractive thing to do. Most importantly, he gave Garlin work where he could clearly see a tangible, visible benefit (snow off the sidewalk, or a clean, weed-free driveway).

I learned quickly, and one day decided that, at the age of five, it was time for young Garlin to start making up his bed. The first day he made his bed, he did a terrible job. "Good start!" I said to encourage him. "Next time, let's pull the corners a little bit more." I showed him how to do just that. By the end of the week, Garlin was making up his bed with military precision. He was so proud and I was thankful that this was one less daily job for me to perform.

Later, as Garlin got older, Garlin Sr. taught him, and got him involved in, the wide range of chores required to run our house. Cutting the grass was especially important. Garlin couldn't play football or basketball with his friends until that chore was completed. His friends did not have yard chores, but they wanted their friend to play. So guess what? The friends decided to help Garlin with the lawn so he could hurry up and play. The boys didn't even consider "helping" work. They just wanted their friend Garlin to be free! Garlin Sr. and I still chuckle about how motivated they were.

That's important. Give your child meaningful work as early as possible, and show them how to do that work. They will see themselves as valued, contributing members to the family. This is a good way for them to ultimately enter the larger society.

The Messages You Send

In the 1960s, the Governor of Michigan, George Romney, claimed that he had been "brainwashed" by the U.S. military to support the Vietnam War. That claim focused the nation's attention on the concept. Brainwashing has multiple meanings. In one sense, it is a "coercive persuasion," or forcefully feeding a certain viewpoint/perspective to an individual, in essence making them at least *say* they believe what you are saying, is one definition. Another definition is "instilling certain attitudes and beliefs in a person" (Wikipedia).

I would suggest to you that part of your job as parents is to "brainwash" your child. Not by using unethical techniques, but by repeating the messages you want to impress upon them over and over again. If we don't set the tone for what our children learn and believe, then who will? We set the standard, and our standards are the bar against which our children should measure everything else. If someone (such as a teacher, a so-called friend, a neighbor, or even a relative) tells your child they are ignorant or stupid, that message should bounce right off their wall of instilled messages that you have told them from years before. Your child should be given enough positive messaging from you, over and over again, to reject messages inconsistent with their internal programming, their internal core values and principals, as fashioned by you.

When Garlin started pre-school, this is how we explained this major event in his life to him: "You're going to school because you are SO smart!" He was excited to go, and he believed he was something called "smart," which

27

was apparently something good because of the way his mom and dad said the word. When he came home with his projects and his verbal reports of what he did in school each day, we got excited with him.

In other words, we "brainwashed" him by telling him over and over how great school was, how smart he was, how much fun learning was, how terrific his teachers were, how nice his friends at school were, and on and on.

Guess what? He believed us.

At dinner time, we sat down and ate together. Garlin's place was right in the middle of our two chairs, and the three of us would discuss the day. We always included him in dinner discussions, and we let him know through our conversation and body language that his day was important too.

This had long-term benefits. As Garlin got older, and we asked about his day, about his friends, even about girlfriends, he didn't think we were nosy parents. It was completely normal for us to ask him those questions. If you ask questions while they're young, your child may clam up later, but they'll probably tell you enough to give you the insight you need. "What happened at karate? How many laps did you swim during swim class? How was it? Did you struggle or was it fun? What did you do? Who was there?" Talk all the time about things going on in your child's world, so they will be accustomed to and comfortable with sharing.

The converse was true as well. We allowed Garlin to ask us questions about our lives apart from him, and we answered them fully. At age appropriate levels, he understood where we worked, names and sometimes faces associated with co-workers and/or friends, and at a high level, things that were going on at our respective workplaces. Church has always played a tremendous role in our family life. So of course he understood things that were going on at that venue as well. This sharing process has to be mutual to be meaningful.

You should nurture in your child a sense of concern for the entire family. If you are people of faith, ask your child to pray for you and others around them. They should understand that you are human too, and have needs. I am not saying that you are to unburden your troubles and woes on your children—far from it! Instead, just let them know that Mom and Dad struggle sometimes with things going on in their lives, too, such as their attitudes, finances or job issues. We have heard, haven't we, that God hears children's sincere, innocent prayers before anyone else's? That itself is a "brainwashing" message!

Why not say: "Mommy's not feeling well today; will you be sure to ask God to make me better?" Or, "Daddy was kind of angry at somebody at work. Pray that God will help me forgive them." Simple things like that, that they can understand and ask you about later, keep you on your toes as well!

Sharing like this with your children teaches them empathy and lets them know that there is more to this life than oneself. There are other ways as well. Whenever I sent sympathy cards to people, I would let Garlin know: "We're sad about this family's loss, and we want to send something to cheer them up." It is important to model empathy as well as provide opportunities for your child to practice empathy.

Many of the teens who kill, harm or bully others do so because they were never nurtured in empathetic behavior. Teaching empathy is probably one of the most important lessons you can convey to your child.

Gratitude is Fundamental

It is also important to teach your child gratitude. Gratitude is NOT a natural trait! It is acquired by children whose parents direct them very intentionally to ACT in ways that demonstrate gratitude.

"Say thank you."

"Call grandmother and tell her thank you for being the best babysitter in the whole wide world."

"We're writing a thank you note to Auntie. You can decorate it with stickers and write your name here."

"Grandpa gave you such a nice gift. Let's go over and see him so you can give him a big hug. I'm going to call and see if he needs us to pick up anything from the store and bring it to him."

As you demonstrate gratefulness in such concrete ways, the feelings of gratefulness percolate up naturally from your heart. Gratefulness is one of the best ways to inoculate your child against bitterness, depression, and the rudeness that seems to be more prevalent among our teenaged children, many of whom have apparently not acquired this critical trait. Parents, when your child says something or does something nice, be grateful and say, "Thank you," to your child and then, in return, when you say something or do something nice to them or for them, expect them to be grateful and to say, "Thank you" to you as well.

My heart is so saddened when I see ungrateful and thankless children, or even adults for that matter. Teach your children that it is important to be grateful and to show gratitude. Teach them that no one has to do anything for them or give them anything. The best gifts, words, and deeds are done out of love or duty. Teach your child to recognize this and to respect it. Teach them to give and to be gracious in their giving, to enjoy and find pleasure in giving and to enjoy and find pleasure in being grateful when someone blesses them with a gift or performs a deed. Grace and gratitude are ALWAYS in order!

Take an honest look in the mirror. Are you demonstrating gratefulness? When? Do you thank your child? After all, gratefulness and appreciation must be modeled to be demonstrated. This begins in the HOME, and only then outwards to the school, church, extended family, or job. A kind word or an appreciative gesture are always warranted. Ask yourself, "Where can I do better?"

If you are honest and admit that you or your child may have fallen short or missed the mark, practice makes perfect. It's never too late to begin anew. A journey begins with that first step. Model this change of heart and change of behavior, and you will begin to see and feel the grace flowing in your own heart, and manifesting itself in the hearts of your disciplined children.

YOUR HOMEWORK

Help your child find a place where they can practice "inward listening." For infants, it may be a crib or playpen. As they get older, you can begin to communicate to them about a "listening place." This is simply a special space where they can be alone with themselves. Let your child know the purpose of that place. Ask them what they would like to put in their special place. Books or toys, a Bible or another holy book. Let your child choose some special items to put there. List three meaningful "work" assignments you can give to your pre-school child. Think beyond just putting his clothes or toys away—that's something they do for themselves. Instead, think of "work" they can do that will benefit the entire household.

Assignment #1 _____

_____

Assignment #2 _____

_____

Assignment #3 _____

_____

Structured Love in Action—The Pre-School Years

List three "acts of kindness" for someone else that you can do that demonstrate empathy and enlist your child's participation.

Act #1 _____

Act #2 _____

Act #3 _____

List three ways that you have demonstrated appreciation/gratefulness in the past week.

#1 _____

#2 _____

#3 _____

List three ways that you can demonstrate appreciation/gratefulness in the upcoming week.

#1 _____

#2 _____

#3 _____

33

POSITIONING YOUR CHILD FOR SUCCESS

List three ways your child has demonstrated 'unsolicited' appreciation/gratefulness this past week.

    #1_____

    #2_____

    #3_____

List three ways that you can direct your child to demonstrate appreciation/gratefulness in the upcoming week.

    #1_____

    #2_____

    #3_____

List three ways that you might volunteer to enhance your child's class room or school.

    #1_____

    #2_____

    #3_____

THE PRE-SCHOOL LEVEL: SUMMARY OF CRITICAL TASKS

❖ *Stability*—you have to be there for your child, every day—with consistent love, patience, attention and care.

❖ *Embrace multiple interactions/diversity of intimate environments*—so your child can adjust to all kinds of personalities. Make sure the environments are safe, nurturing and loving.

❖ *Help your child become satisfied and comfortable with him/herself*—make sure that your child can self-entertain for periods of time. Stay in their visual line, but maintain space that allows you to do what you need to do around the house. Allow "nothing" time.

❖ *Crazy Love (Is there ever "too much?")*—too much hugging and affection, too much praise (make it specific—not "You're great" but "I really like the way you painted this picture; you used a lot of good color combinations!")

❖ *Fun Learning*—Make a game of everything!

❖ *Brainwash*—if you don't do it, someone else will!

❖ Read to your child and let your child read to you DAILY. Books open up a whole new world and stimulate the imagination.

❖ *Use real words*—don't talk "baby talk" to your children.

❖ *Celebrate accomplishment*—make it a big production; the refrigerator is a great place to put their artwork, awards, or papers that show excellence or improvement.

❖ Make sure you are available to help your child's pre-school teacher.

Partnering With Your Child's Educator

We were fortunate in that Garlin's pre-school required structured parental involvement. But I went a step further. I was always looking around to see what the teacher might need. In most schools, funds are short and so the teacher does not always have everything they would like to provide a maximally enriching educational experience.

This is the question that is music to your child's teacher's ears: "I noticed that you run out of (NAME A PARTICULAR SET OF SUPPLIES) quite often. Would it be helpful if I brought some for the class?" It may be extra pencils, or treats for a special occasion, or reading books, or even empty two-liter bottles to make mini water funnels for an easy science demonstration. You might suggest an even more wide-open question, such as, "Is there anything you need help with?" Later in your child's academic career, it might be community outreach, advocacy with the principal, or securing a career day speaker. You never know how you might assist until you ask.

In summary, at the pre-school level the partnering is very much hands-on. You are there, visible to your child, as well as the teacher. Your child knows that school is something important—not just because you told them, but because you are actively involved and helping.

~

SECTION TWO

Techniques—
What To Do For Your
Child Grade-By-Grade

CHAPTER 4

Elementary School:
"You Have My Name"

"You have my name."

I used the subtitle "You have my name" for this chapter because this is what my husband told Garlin when he was in elementary school.

"You have my name." When my husband said that to Garlin, he meant it. The statement is rich with meaning, a richness that grows every year as children learn just how significant it is to bear the family name. It is a concept you should introduce to your child at the elementary school level. At this level, they are cognitively able to grasp it.

I look back on the father-to-son mentoring between Garlin and our son with total joy. I watched my husband turn my little boy into a man, and I am grateful for the time they spent together one-on-one; then as well as today. Garlin Sr. taught him the importance of work, and they worked side-by-side. "Man, come on," Garlin Sr. would say. "We have to pick up people for church" (or whatever act of service he might be involved in at the time). Garlin Sr. began involvement in his son's early basketball and baseball life as a Parks and Recreation Department coach for the elementary grades. In later years, he moved to the sidelines as an excited and supportive father and "sideline coach." He rarely missed a game or a practice.

As a mother, I found that I could mentor Garlin as well. Those elusive emotional qualities—of gratitude, empathy, and commitment—were my strong character traits and pretty easy for me to model. I was the one who made sure that he wrote the thank-you notes, and Garlin went with me to conduct 'in home' Bible studies with the sick and shut-in.

Garlin Sr. and I were a "tag team" of sorts. We each had our unique way of connecting with and teaching our child. I call it "Mentoring-Plus"—a way to show them by doing, and a way to build relationship and facilitate communication. That "Plus" is the extra hands-on, alongside care that a parent or other mentor gives. It tells the child that he can always rely on the mentor or parent's intimate involvement, consistent presence, comfort, and constant teaching.

"Whenever I played a game," Garlin reflectively shares now, "I knew my Dad was there. He had a spot on the floor where he always stood, and I knew that if I looked at that spot anytime during the game, I'd see him." It was so important to him to know that.

My husband drove one of our church buses to pick up the elderly and handicapped members of our church, and he frequently took Garlin with him on his route. It was a very special time of bonding. Garlin was expected to help the elderly and disabled to get on and off the bus. He didn't mind at all, because he was with his dad, and he saw his dad doing the very same things he was telling his son to do. By the time he was eight, Garlin was helping older ladies onto the bus all by himself. It was a great way for him to learn compassion and respect for the elderly or disabled, and to learn how to be tender, kind, and patient with elderly individuals who may have a hard time hearing, seeing or walking.

Modeling is so important at this age. With our extended family, Garlin helped his grandparents and his aunts with whatever they needed. Basement clean-out? They called on Garlin. Something on a ledge too far away to reach? Garlin was tall; he could get it for them. Doors opened? Garlin was right there. Leaves to be raked? Gutters to clean? Snow to shovel? He was there for that too. Eventually, he would call them to see if there was anything they needed. He became a very popular nephew and grandson! And even more, he was visibly proud that he could be such an important and contributing member of the family.

The other benefits? How about patience when you have to interact with an older person to clearly understand what they need from you? Maybe they talk a bit more slowly than the parents do? Maybe they don't move quite as fast? Then, there is the learning of respect as you have to exercise that patience and perhaps ask again what they need because you were not quite clear the first time. Those are critical life lessons, and those are the lessons that Garlin had to execute over and over again until they became second nature to him.

We also took Garlin to our church or organizational meetings. We started getting him involved early. By the time he was six years old, he was helping by passing out papers, counting the number of people present in the room, and whatever he could do to tangibly help that was appropriate to his age. Again, just like pre-school, we were gradually introducing work into his life as he moved from elementary to high school. You don't want your child to graduate from high school or college and see work as a foreign country! In our household, "going to work" could be many things, from a job to a church function or a community event. In our home, work was always a positive event, never a negative one. It was a time to be excited about the possibilities that each new day held, and an opportunity to feel good about getting something done.

That's Mentoring-Plus. A hands-on way of teaching by doing WITH your child, rather than merely talking TO your child about what he should be doing.

With all of this learning and mentoring, our next step was to give him increasing opportunities to exercise maturity, one small step at a time. When Garlin was about seven, Garlin Sr. had to go on a business trip. "You're the man of the house while I'm gone," he told our son. Garlin took his role very seriously. At bedtime, I began turning out the downstairs lights when Garlin stopped me. "Mom, I'll shut down, you go up to bed." I even let him tuck me in. He was learning. You might think this was a little thing, but we were *building* on what we were trying to teach him about responsibility and about leadership. He was proud to be taking care of me while his dad was out of town and I was more than pleased with his committed effort. He was mimicking the things he had seen his dad do to shut down our home at night. Put away the evening's trash. Close and check doors, turn off lights, tuck everyone into bed for the evening. Protect the home and the loved ones inside. Isn't imitation the greatest form of flattery? Yes, Garlin had watched his father do these things for years and now when his chance came around, he performed his role with military precision. I was happy to play my role and let my little guy 'protect and care' for me.

Speak Up!

Part of taking these small steps involved teaching Garlin to communicate. We began right at the dinner table, where he learned to talk freely with two adults who loved him. He spoke, also, with his extended family members who listened to pretty much everything he had to say. It was time to continue the forward progress by initiating him into the world of public speaking.

Our children are often very shy about speaking in public, and they have to be helped to move beyond their fears. The world they will enter as adults will require that they be able to speak clearly and persuasively. If they want to be leaders and advance in their chosen profession, it is imperative that they be able to speak well. And you as the parent should provide ample public speaking opportunities for your child.

There are many outlets where your child can practice their public speaking skills. If you are part of a church or faith-based institution, there are the traditional Christmas, Easter, Sunday School, Bible Study, or other religious and cultural programs in which your child may participate. There are also the requisite school events, youth community theatre programs, clubs and many opportunities where your child can learn this important skill.

Garlin participated in church programs all the time, even as a pre-schooler. Whenever he had a speaking part in one of those programs, we'd tell him:

"Stand up straight."

"Use your outside voice. No one can enjoy what you have to say if they can't hear you."

"Hold your head up; you haven't done anything to be ashamed of!"

"If you have something to say, say it and be proud of it."

"EVERYBODY wants to hear what you have to say!"

Please note the last phrase. Isn't that brainwashing? Yes! Remember, it's okay to brainwash. After all, they'll be brainwashed by the media, by their teachers, by their peers and their peers' parents, and by people you might not necessarily want them to hear from. You want to get your subliminal and not-so-subliminal messages in as much, and as early, as possible.

To drive home our messages about the importance of these public speaking presentations, we would have Garlin stand up against the door under the doorknob so he could practice with a straight back. We would also have him memorize his speaking part. There was no reading from cue cards with us! If your children can memorize popular song lyrics almost instantaneously, they can certainly memorize their lines for a school or church program. You may have to do a little extra, maybe turn their lines into a song so that they can remember. But that's okay. The bottom line is, practice makes perfect.

We tried to put Garlin into a variety of performance situations—church, community groups, and other public opportunities where he might not know as many of the people in the audience. This minimizes inhibitions, and reduces the natural propensity towards stage fright. As an added benefit, once he had a few public speaking presentations under his belt, Garlin was poised and never even developed a fear of public speaking. We told him he could do it. He believed us and moved forward with gusto, delivering his lines in a play or reciting parts on a program with enthusiasm and great confidence.

Setting Expectations

A little later, when Garlin was in the third or fourth grade, my husband had "the talk." (No, not THAT talk. This was the talk about the future and what Garlin could expect in planning and preparing for his future.)

"Son, you come from good stock; you have my name," Garlin Sr. began. "The Lord has blessed you, and you can go far in this world. But understand this, *on your 18th birthday, you will have a new address.* You will not live here. I don't want there to be any confusion or misunderstanding. You can prepare yourself for a good and positive future by living in someone's college dorm or you can be about the business of making it on your own out on the street. The road of life is yours. You can go up or down it. The choice is yours. If you play your cards right, you'll be in a college dorm trying to prepare a good future for yourself."

My husband continued. "You have a fine mind. We don't expect you to get all A's all the time, but we do expect you to do your very best at all times…and unfortunately for you, we will *know* when you have done your best and when you have not."

"And oh by the way, if you're not planning to be living in a college dorm," Garlin Sr. concluded, "you better make enough money at McDonald's to take care of your mama."

This was all about setting expectations for our son. Your child's success does NOT happen by osmosis; it takes planned, deliberate, and concerted effort by both you and your child. I believe that one of the most important actions you can take, very early in your young child's life, is to clearly state your expectations and vision for their future. I believe that some children don't leave home after graduation from high school because, in many instances, no one ever told them that they had to. So these children see no value in working hard to prepare themselves to enter college or a trade school or to find a job. Home is comfortable. Home is familiar. Home is fun. Home is free. Given all of this, these children, in their immaturity, may find no need for things to change. The child's plan might be to "live upstairs" forever. If you as a parent don't want that to happen, I'd seriously suggest communicating a very different scenario with your children and to make your expectations crystal clear.

You and Your Child's School: Getting Off to a Good Start

We started thinking about where we would live during Garlin's early school years. We considered several different options. By the time he was in the first grade, we made the decision to enlarge our concept of where we might live, and began looking at suburbs around Detroit. But we didn't make a decision until we visited the area schools.

I made an appointment with the principal of one of the Detroit suburban elementary schools. I gave him the address of the house we were considering, and told him I just wanted to make sure that the house was in his district.

Of course, I could have found that out by other means. I didn't need the principal to give me that information. So why did I do it this way?

It's simple. I knew Garlin was going to be the only African American in his class, and I wanted to make sure that the principal: 1) knew who we were, and 2) and most importantly, clearly understood our commitment to remaining involved in Garlin's education.

Besides, it is important to double check. Sometimes a house is right at the border between two communities, and a family purchases a house assuming that their child will be in one school district only to find out too late, after the new home is purchased, that it is in another, perhaps less desirable, school district.

We confirmed that the house we were looking at was indeed in the school district we were considering, and purchased our new home and moved in on May 1st, so that Garlin could meet and get to know his new classmates over the summer. This turned out to be a very wise decision because Garlin was able to learn his new neighborhood and meet new friends over the summer. He was then able to begin the next school year familiar with his new surroundings, at ease with his new friends, and confident that he was ready and able to learn at school.

I really appreciated the way Garlin was challenged by his classmates. They expected one another to do well and when one faltered, they gathered close to try and analyze what was causing the problem. I can remember one of my earliest recollections of this. Garlin was in the third grade and the children were learning and practicing timed multiplication drills. His little circle of four or five boys all expected to get all of the problems correct in the allotted drill time. All of a sudden, Garlin started getting 94 or 95 on his quizzes, instead of the expected 100%. I tell you, these young men thought that this was a serious problem that had to be solved, and solved immediately! I was so tickled. His friends watched him to try and figure out what was going wrong. They knew that he knew the answers but they couldn't figure out why he was losing time during the math drill. Voila! The boys figured it out. Shazaam! They solved the mystery. These little third graders figured out that my son was putting his pencil down after a certain time between problems. This was causing him to lose precious seconds during the math drill and therefore, causing him to waste time and fall behind. Baamm! Problem solved. Garlin stopped putting his pencil down, regained those precious seconds, and was back to scoring 100% on his math drills once again.

I love this story because it is representative of the commitment his friends had to being good students and to ensuring that all in their group succeeded. This was an example of positive peer pressure and positive peer role modeling. Garlin remained friends with many of these young men and throughout their academic careers, most lost neither that zest for learning nor the quest for excellence. As a parent I certainly appreciated the adventure, not to mention the positive peer pressure.

Remember a little earlier that I mentioned how important it was to teach your child how to open up and freely share what's going on in their lives? And how important being together as a family during the dinner hour was? Let me demonstrate how that worked in one very concrete way. "Mommie, I got sent to the corner in Art class today," Garlin said at the dinner table one evening. He was in the fourth grade. We knew that Garlin had a brand new art teacher at school and that something strange had to be going on because Art was one of his favorite classes.

"You did? Why?" we asked.

"Teacher said I was talking."

"Were you talking?" we asked.

"Yes."

"Well Garlin, were you talking when the teacher asked you not to talk?"

"No," he answered.

We didn't ask any more questions.

Because of our ongoing dinner chats, I knew that this was the first time this had happened. Art class was held once each week and I decided to pay a visit to Garlin's art class the very next time it was in session.

First, I called the principal. "I'd like to observe my son's Art class," I told him. "I'll be coming in tomorrow." I also called the art teacher to let her know that I would be visiting my son's next class session as well. I didn't tell my son that I was coming.

It took me all of ten minutes to see that the art teacher had absolutely no classroom management skills. The kids were all over the place. It was bedlam, and she was merely a passive agent. She never told the students when they were to listen and when they were free to quietly chat. Finally, after what I can only describe as prolonged periods of utter chaos, she would get frustrated and just start sending various kids to the corner randomly.

I didn't say a word. I simply observed the goings on of that particular art session. Afterwards, I immediately went back to the principal and recounted what I had just observed.

But I did more than just tell the story. I requested a meeting with the art teacher, the principal, and myself. I waited until there was a break in her schedule, and then asked her some pointed questions.

"I'm curious, did you send my son to the corner?"

"Yes," she replied.

"Did Garlin disobey you?"

"No."

"So why did you send him to the corner?"

"He was talking."

"Did you tell him NOT to talk?"

"Well, no."

"Was he the only child talking at that particular time?"

"No."

"So please help me understand why a child who was never instructed NOT to talk, began talking—this is an art class and it is not uncommon for child to chat as they work, is it not?—was all of a sudden sent to the corner, without prior warning that his behavior was somehow out of line? I'll ask you again, why was my son singled out to be sent to the corner?"

"The children were getting noisy."

"May I tell you what I observed today? I observed a lack of classroom management. The children were never told at what times they should sit and listen attentively to you for instruction, versus a time when they may quietly work and chat amongst themselves, awaiting a cue from the teacher to again stop and pay attention to the teacher. Instead, what I witnessed was utter classroom chaos, and when you became frustrated, students were randomly ordered to the corner without regard to which children were major or minor disrupters of the classroom."

I shared with both the art teacher and the principal that I would not allow my son to be treated in such a fashion. If he did something wrong, I expected him to accept the consequences of those actions. But I was not going to allow him to be unfairly sent to punishment corners just because the teacher did not have control of her classroom. No, I was not going to tolerate that behavior from this teacher or any other person. She admitted that Garlin had NOT disobeyed her, yet he was sent to corner. That would NOT be happening to my son again, even if it meant that I needed to come and sit in the back of the classroom during all of the art sessions.

Suffice it to say that these comments solicited the appropriate response. The principal to his credit assured me that it would NOT be necessary for me to take time off of my job to sit in the back of Garlin's art class. He stated that he knew Garlin well and the type of student that he was and that he had never known a teacher to state that he misbehaved in their classroom. The art teacher agreed. The principal shared that he would address the lack of classroom management matter as a training issue and that going forward none of the students were going to be indiscriminately sent to a corner. He asked me if his plan was acceptable to me. I assured him that my son loved art class and that, as long as he was treated fairly, I would never have a problem. But if he was treated unfairly, I was willing to do whatever it took to rectify the problem. The young teacher then asked me an interesting question:

"Why does this even matter to you? It's just an art class."

I responded: "Everything that happens to our son is important to us. We care about every single aspect of our son's educational experience, and being sent to a corner for no reason could diminish his self-esteem, and under absolutely no circumstance will we sit idly by and let that happen, ever." She stated that she hadn't thought about her actions from that perspective and truly meant no harm. I believed her and stated that I would love to see things turn around for the good of my son and all of the other children.

That was the first and only time that I had to visit any of Garlin's schools for disciplinary issues. I felt good about letting an educator know that parents do care about all aspects of their child's education, and about helping a principal address an important class management challenge in his school.

Under the tutelage of the principal and perhaps others, the new art teacher learned how to manage her classroom. Garlin was never sent back to the corner again. And guess what? He got an "A" in art. What's more, in 2000, when he graduated, the principal came to his open house at our home. And Garlin is still pretty good at art today.

What's the lesson here? As the parent, you establish your ground rules for each teacher. Let them know that they should contact you immediately if there is a problem. Be open to the idea that the teacher just wants your child to be the best that they can be, but make sure you observe him or her in action so that you can make that determination yourself. If the teacher is correct in disciplining your child, support them 100% and administer your own brand of correction at home as well. But, if you find any hint of unfairness, address it firmly and in no uncertain terms. And always, always keep the dialogue positive and constructive. With that strategy, you will find, as I did, that you will spend progressively less and less time in school regarding disciplinary matters concerning your child.

Parents, you must be your child's primary advocate at this level, usually much more than in the earlier grades. After all, when they are in pre-school, they're cute, and the teachers hug them and love them like parents. But around ages 8-10, that typically disappears, and you see students starting to exert themselves more and teachers having to take control...not always in the most effective ways.

So we've talked about advocacy, and about the importance of staying in touch with your child's school day. Now I'm going to cover the other side of that coin: proactive service.

"Did You Help Your Mama?"

"Proactive service" is the term I use to describe Garlin's move to the next level of development. This phase has to start early. As early as pre-school, we let him know that his

56

job was to go to school. Now, it was:

"Did you help your mama?"

Garlin Sr. asked our son that question all the time. If they were home and they heard me driving into the garage, he let Garlin know that he should automatically go to the car to see if I needed any help. Garlin was always directed to move *to* the work, not *away* from it. He was to serve proactively; to actually look and observe where he might be of help. That instills responsibility and sets up lifetime habits that will sustain them in their family as well as their work relationships. I expect that Garlin's wife loves him because he will, out of habit, look for ways to help her. His boss and co-workers will respect him for the same reasons. Because he has been educated and trained to be a giving individual, his "doing" will be rewarded with favor and blessings.

Expectations do not come by osmosis. You have to spell them out to your child as soon as they can understand, and repeat them often, in order for them to stick.

Neither does your child's sense of security come by osmosis. And that's why, at the same time that you are instilling a sense of responsibility, you should also be your child's first advocate and cheerleader when they are doing what is right…and correcting them constructively when they are not.

When bonded together correctly, advocacy and responsibility are a powerful two-sided coin.

YOUR HOMEWORK

1. If your child is having problems behaviorally or academically in a class or classes, make an appointment to visit the school to observe exactly what is happening. Determine whether your child needs to be disciplined, or if there is something going on with the teacher. Be objective, and don't automatically blame the teacher/administration for inappropriate behavior on the part of your child.

2. Make a list of key household tasks for which your child will be responsible, and hold them to those responsibilities with no exceptions.

    _____

    _____

    _____

    _____

    _____

    _____

    _____

THE ELEMENTARY LEVEL: A SUMMARY OF CRITICAL TASKS

Preparation Strategies

❖ Communication—begin introducing public speaking experiences for your child—oratorical contests, church, community and school opportunities, school-wide programs, encourage them to be on Student Council or participate in other leadership roles, practice oral book reports, etc.

❖ Play counting games when you go on trips to the grocery store or mall. Play games which require your child to actively participate in keeping track of the cost of various goods or services against a set budget amount. When you go to purchase new carpet for a room in your home or the entire house, let your child help figure out the total square footage of the room(s), number of feet or yards required, price per yard and the total bill. You can find any number of opportunities to introduce and reinforce math concepts, and your child will need math to be successful today!

❖ Expectations—create a clear vision and guidance about your child's future.

❖ Household basics—don't be a chauvinist! Boys have to know as much as girls do. This includes bed-making, cleaning his room, washing his clothes and dishes, and dusting, as well as garbage takeout, snow-shoveling and leaf-raking.

❖ Service—emphasize service and demonstrate helpfulness to the immediate, as well as extended, family as well as friends. Helping should start to become automatic. You should not have to call your child out to bring groceries in when you come back from the grocery store. They should be at the car and ready when you come back.

❖ Goals—teach age-appropriate self-sufficiency and allow your child to make age-appropriate choices.

Partnering With Your Child's Educator

❖ Be your child's advocate. Visit the class frequently to get the real "scoop" on what's going on. The best schools allow unannounced visits to allow parents a clear picture of a realistic school day.

❖ Let teachers and administrators know you're there to partner with them in your child's education. Here is your suggested 'stump speech':

"Nothing is more important to us than our child's well-being and we care about everything related to his/her development. We are involved parents. We are sending you a respectful child; if that doesn't line up with their behavior, please communicate that to us immediately. We look

forward to partnering with you in our child's education."

❖ Respectfully get to know the administration, as well as the teachers, and allow them to get to know you. If you want to make sure your child is in a school where you are positive about the educational staff and leadership, you must make an informed opinion. You must be fully informed about, and conversant with, each teacher's curriculum, classroom management rules, strategies, and expectations of the students.

What if your child is struggling?

This is no time to sit back and hope that things will get better. It's a very sensitive time, because your child's self-esteem may hang in the balance. You must maintain the delicate tightrope walk between realism and optimism.

There is a way to successfully do this. Identify and document the deficiency, push for the correct diagnosis, and then document the plan and your child's progress. Start with the teacher, then the counselor, and ultimately the principal. Take advantage of the community service organizations to which they may refer you. There is help available as long as you let it be known that you are open and willing to receive it. The school personnel can't help solve a problem that they are not aware of!

Then of course, you'll need their assistance in identifying the source of the challenge. Is it simply that your child needs academic assistance and extra tutoring? Do you need to impose more discipline? More love? A better study area? Something physical like eye glasses? Or are there other, more deep-seated emotional reasons for their struggles? Again, don't be afraid to be honest.

Awareness is critical. Here's a news flash: As wonderful as you are, you don't know everything—no one person does–but you are responsible, as a parent, for finding out the answer and accepting the criticism. You may not want to hear that you need to turn the TV off and stop using it as a babysitter. You may not want to hear that you have to say "no" more frequently to your child. But you may need to hear it. You may need help getting your house in order. It may need slight tweaking or it may require a complete overhaul. But whatever you do, *get the help you need.*

If your child is struggling, it's especially important to understand the problem areas, and to document their progress. Children in real or perceived crisis especially need this. Here is a possible script:

"This is where you are; but we're going to work to do better."

This statement gives intrinsic value. You are demonstrating confidence in your child's ability to accept and respond to assistance, giving importance to both internal and external sources.

"You're struggling in math; now we're going to ask the school for help."

Document that too. You'll be able to show progress to your child and find out from the teacher how to proceed, and that's extremely important.

When your child is struggling, it's 'all hands on deck.' Chart their progress, and put your child's plans right in their portfolio (See Section 4).

CHAPTER 5

Middle School:
They STILL Need You

Parents, get a grip. If you thought parenting was challenging up to this point, you're in for another level! Parenting is all-consuming from here on.

From now until your child graduates from high school, forget about having a life. You need to be on school committees. You need to volunteer for as much as you can at your child's school. You will have to be there for them. Engaged parents allow the child to see their parents' words in action.

Now at times, they won't necessarily like it. At least, they won't tell you they like it. They have to keep up that "front," especially for their friends. Don't listen to them when they tell you they don't want you to "be there."

I know of one mother who has a lifelong regret. Her son made the eighth grade basketball team, and he literally begged her not to come to his first game. "Please, Mom, I'll just be distracted, and I want to play my best." That was his line. She reluctantly agreed.

At that game, he scored twenty points.

Years later, he said to his mom, "I really wished you had been there for my first game."

She was incredulous. "You begged me not to come! I was respecting your wishes!" she protested. He had to admit she was right.

But is it worth it to be right? Or is it better to be *wise*?

Your child will appreciate any effort you make to be in their lives. They may never tell you. But it's important that you know.

There is one critical difference between that example and your involvement at the middle school level, however. You don't need to be in the classroom with your child. So, no more sitting in back of class. It embarrasses your child and keeps them from growing.

Hopefully, you've instilled in them the idea that respect for the teacher and for classroom rules is paramount, and they're actually more concerned about getting in trouble with you than they are of getting in trouble with the teacher. Now, you may be in the hallways, volunteering as a hall monitor. You may be stamping hands at sports events in which your child is involved. Or you may be president of the local school community organization. So you are present, but you're not in your child's face all the time. The bottom line is that you are involved, but you're gradually giving your child larger wings and more independence.

Take it slow. It's going to be a long ride.

And while you may not be in the classroom, it is important to make yourself visible to the infrastructure of educational staff that will be impacting your child's life. You may not be in love with each and every one of them. But you do have to get along with all of them.

This is Exploration Time!

Now is the time to get your child involved in a range of activities—academic, non-academic, and community service. You should be earnestly building their portfolio in all of these areas, and for several reasons:

To help them discover what their interests are. How will your child know what they want to do if they don't even know what's out there? Is there a Great Books program at your library on Saturdays? Take them! Do they hate it? What about math or science enrichment? The tuba? Piano? What about dance, acting or poetry classes?

Or what if they don't want to do anything? Not an option! I know one mom whose son told her that he had no

67

intentions of participating in the program that she talked to him about. "You're right. You *have* no intentions. I will be doing *all* of your intending for you until you graduate from high school." She was right. The reason children have parents is because they are children! They often don't know what they want OR need yet...and we are shortchanging them if we do not think strategically about what is best for them, and how to achieve it.

To keep them busy. My grandmother always said, "The idle mind is the devil's workshop." Children should not be sitting in their rooms on their laptops or cell phones that you can't see, or spending most of their free time at the mall. Yes, they do need "down time." A 12-year-old should have time to be 12. But, they also need to be led and guided by you into the potential that you know is in them. Just try. Try out programs on them and see what works...and what does not. Nothing beats a failure but a try.

To instill in them the value of service. The world needs people who will give of themselves to others in need; human nature, left to itself, will focus pretty much completely on itself. Your child is part of a greater world, and needs to see that something they have to contribute. When you expose them to service, your child will benefit as they see others whose needs are greater than their own, and ultimately the world will benefit from a functioning adult who has something to offer to society.

To create a "track record" for your child, and ensure that they are competitive with other students at college, scholarship, internship and work time. My son's portfolio for just one of the scholarships he won was about two inches thick. More on this later, but we listed every organization for which he volunteered, included thank you and commendation letters for his service and accomplishments, and even tucked in local newspaper articles on him from our community paper. We had pages and pages of the work he'd done in various academic and sports activities, including awards, welcome letters, and program accomplishments. These days, there are thousands of parents doing the same. They are offering to those gatekeepers of the academic and work worlds that, "My child is well-socialized, academically adept, and ready to take his/her place with your institution." How will your child match up?

Where to start? Here are just a few places to investigate:

- Local Library

- Local colleges and universities/community colleges

- School counselor

- Public recreational facilities or local YMCA/YWCA

It's okay to ask open-ended questions. "I'm looking for a good summer activity for my daughter/son. What do you have available?" You will find fee-based programs, but you'll also find a lot of activities where you can participate free of charge or at a very affordable cost.

Do this, and your children will be surprised at what they find out about themselves...and YOU will be surprised at what they do with the experiences that you provide for them.

POSITIONING YOUR CHILD FOR SUCCESS

Don't Be a Jerk

I know it sounds harsh, but I'm trying to make a point. You will not win on your child's behalf if you try to bully or coerce their teachers, their administrators, or their coaches. I had to learn that you catch more flies with honey than vinegar, and you will have to learn that very same lesson. Is your child not getting enough playing time on the basketball/volleyball/baseball team? Tough! They'll need to learn to handle adversity and disappointment. Maybe it is favoritism, or, even worse, racism. But your inappropriate intervention often ends up with your child paying the price, with the friction and animosity often created when parents insert themselves in ways that they shouldn't. Plus, if your child doesn't get practice handling the adversities of life here, at this age, how will they be equipped to handle it later, when they become adults and *real* adversity hits?

After all, what is the end game? Is it that your child gets everything he or she wants, or is it that your child gets prepared for real life? I'm sure I don't have to answer that for you.

This is really important. A lot of parents play it down, but you should be careful not to embarrass your child at this age. It's so hard for them to fit in, and the way you carry yourself, dress, and behave can potentially be a source of deep frustration. Do not yell or scream at your child in public; they could actually be ostracized because of something that you do or say, and the humiliation can cut deep and last long. We must be sensitive as parents, and not cause our children discomfort that is fully avoidable.

70

We teach our children to honor their parents, but it's a two-way street. Conduct yourself as a parent such that you are worthy of your child's honor.

> *Parents, do not treat your children in such a way as to make them angry. Instead, bring them up with Christian discipline and instruction.*
>
> ~Ephesians 6:4 (GNT)

> *Fathers, do not irritate and provoke your children to anger [do not exasperate them to resentment], but rear them [tenderly] in the training and discipline and the counsel and admonition of the Lord.*
>
> ~ Ephesians 6:4 *Amplified Bible*

> *And now a word to you parents. Don't keep on scolding and nagging your children, making them angry and resentful. Rather, bring them up with the loving discipline the Lord himself approves, with suggestions and godly advice.*
>
> ~Ephesians 6:4 (TLB)

Always an Exception to the Rule

Garlin was a member of his middle school's basketball team, and was also a member of a community league team. The school coach did not know that many of his team members also played for the community team. When Garlin's community team won their league championship, the school coach saw the newspaper article and, in a fit of

71

pique, summarily suspended every one of his players who also played for the other team for the remainder of the season.

In this instance, I *had* to be a busybody, intrusive parent. A group of parents protested the suspension vociferously, yet respectfully, and our sons ended up only suspended for a few games.

Nothing should keep you away when your child's name, or when equity and fairness, are in question.

Remember Garlin Sr.'s words to Garlin when he was a little boy? "You have my name." The Scriptures tell us that a person's name is the most valuable possession they have. It's better than silver or gold. Unfair treatment sullies your child's name, and it must *always* be addressed.

> *If you must choose, take a good name rather than great riches; for to be held in loving esteem is better than silver and gold.*
>
> ~Proverbs 22:1 (TLB)

> *A good name is more desirable than great wealth. Respect is better than silver or gold.*
>
> ~Proverbs 22:1 (God's Word)

> *A GOOD name is rather to be chosen than great riches, and loving favor rather than silver and gold.*
>
> ~Proverbs 22:1 *Amplified Bible*

It's important to know when you can break the "non-intervention" rule. It's just as important to understand how to do that respectfully and in the right spirit. You can express any message you wish; it's *how* you do it that matters.

Your Bank of Favor

Part of having a good name involves building a bank of goodwill. There is a tremendous benefit to your child being known as a strong and respectful student. There is a tremendous benefit to your family when your school and teachers know that you are an involved, "partnering" parent. Having a reputation for being kind, fair, honest and intelligent parents doesn't hurt either.

Your child's good name can prevent them from the danger of false accusations. With a good name, they are less likely to be grouped with the kids in the class who are acting in unruly ways.

The path of favor has proven to be a good one for my family.

In the late 1990s, the DAPCEP program sent out an invitation to ten school principals. They had decided to launch a K-3 (Kindergarten through Third Grade) pilot program to interest young students in mathematics and science. What types of families do you think DAPCEP asked these principals for?

"Send us the names of three to five of your best families whose children will be in Kindergarten next year."

They didn't ask the principals for the five best students. They asked for the five best *families*. The families with the best or "good names," of course, were the ones selected to participate in the pilot program. These families had stellar reputations for parental involvement and a family culture of responsibility and respect. DAPCEP structured this particular program to require intensive family participation in order to be effective.

The program was a phenomenal success. Consistently, more than 90% of DAPCEP participants enroll in college once they graduate from high school, and as many as 60-80% of college graduates who participated in DAPCEP work in engineering and technical fields.

See what a good name can do?

You can add to your family's good name at school by having your child offer ways to help his or her class. "I've got an uncle who's a Tuskegee Airman and former Army officer and he can come and present at school," or, "I have extra construction paper," or "My dad can help paint the school." Offer to participate in your school's career day, or serve as a chaperone on a field trip or at a dance. Or you might volunteer to be a hall, playground or lunch monitor. By doing that, you transfer favor from you to your child and that is a gift.

Safety is Paramount

Remember the Catholic priest scandal? Part of the reason that countless children were subjected to tragic, life-damaging abuse is that parents were much too trusting. In middle school, just like in elementary school, Garlin never went to anything unless one of us was there with him. He couldn't go to sleepovers if we didn't know the parents personally. Some might say that was going overboard, but how could we possibly be comfortable with Garlin's safety if we didn't know what kind of character the parents possessed? There are parents, you know, who allow their children and friends to engage in underage drinking. There are parents, you know, who abuse drugs and leave their kids alone, or worse.

Now, we had absolutely no problem letting Garlin's friends come over for sleepovers at our home. That's the flip side. You don't just tell your child they can't do something; you have to offer an acceptable alternative. That prevents an unhappy child from becoming a sneaky child who tries to do exactly what you tell them they can't do because nothing else is available for them.

We were also the first to agree to chaperone. We know many parents who shied away from that; too "inconvenient," they would say. "Let the other parent do it." That was not us. We understood that if we chaperone, we could ensure that our behavioral standards were being met…and we could impress upon our child our expectations, and make sure that those expectations became a habit for them.

Good habits, just like bad ones, are hard to break. If you've been doing right since infancy, because your parents have enforced it lovingly and in an atmosphere of acceptance and yes, fun, you will typically find no need to break that pattern once your parents give you increasing freedom and independence. At the very least, this prior training will enhance wise decisions and choices. As parents, this is the best we can hope for.

Create a protective cocoon around your child. Notice I said protective, not smothering. That's what I meant earlier in this chapter when I talked about the next level of involvement; where you're not hovering directly around your child, but you are there as a more distant observer and protector. And you're only protecting them from danger to their bodies, their spirits, and their reputations, not from life's everyday disappointments and bumps and bruises!

Extracurricular…Math?

Extracurricular activities are not just for athletics and music. In the fall of the year that Garlin entered the sixth grade, I signed him up for an academic enrichment course called "pre-engineering math." It sounded heavy, but it was really a pre-algebra class. The three hour class was held on Saturday mornings at Wayne State University.

"Mom, I don't want to go to class on Saturday mornings," Garlin told me.

Was I listening to him? No. I cared too much about my child to allow him to dictate, at 12 years of age, what course his life is going to take. He's much too young to do that. And all the other parents who dragged their children to Wayne State University on Saturday mornings obviously felt the same way I did.

So off we went, to something called the DAPCEP Saturday Morning Classes. Garlin, as I mentioned, came along reluctantly at first, but the teacher was a master. Her name was Evelyn Champagne, a middle school math teacher at Higginbotham Middle School in Detroit, and she broke down algebraic concepts to these young people (remember, Algebra is typically taken in 8th or 9th grade) so magnificently that when the children got back to their regular school classes on Monday through Friday, they looked like rocket scientists! Why? They knew their stuff!

Ms. Champagne didn't stop with Saturday mornings. Even though she was a full-time teacher already, she invited her Saturday students to call her at home if they got stuck on their homework, which they did.

So here is my son, looking like a math whiz in middle school. His confidence increased dramatically. Whether he actually got the answers correct or he just knew precisely which questions to ask, the teachers were impressed! And if he got stuck on a homework problem, he could call Ms. Champagne during the week and she would make it crystal clear. Ms. Champagne was an important participant in Garlin's trajectory of academic success and I give her much of the credit. The time we spent on Saturday mornings was a small price to pay. We invested a few hours of time on the weekends for immeasurable benefits when Garlin went to class Monday through Friday.

Please parents, understand your limitations. Do not, I repeat, do not sit down with your child and help them do their math, thinking, "It's only 6th or 7th grade math; I remember this." Often, you certainly do NOT remember this. The math today is much, much different from when you and I were in school. I'm not ashamed to tell you that I might be able to get the right answer to a particular problem, but now there is a different process for getting there and if my child was going to excel he was going to have to learn that new process, not *my* process. If he listened to me, he could get the right answer and still get points taken off because he hadn't followed step one, step two, or step three that the teacher had laid out for him in the new mathematics textbooks. Listen parents: unless this is your forte, just grin and bear it; send them for help!

Having Garlin know how to do his math homework at home in the evenings without me 'sweating' it out with him over the kitchen table was worth its weight in PURE GOLD to me. I sincerely appreciated the fact that he knew what he was doing and was doing it with excellence. This increased his confidence and self-esteem. It also greatly reduced my stress and aggravation because when I came home from a hard day at the office, his homework was done, or nearly completed. Yea! That was worth getting up on Saturday mornings and taking him to DAPCEP, faithfully!

So don't struggle there at the kitchen table with your child; strengthen them academically by participating in these kinds of enrichment programs and get them the exposure they need to be successful.

When the seventh grade rolled around, the DAPCEP catalog listing Saturday class options came in the mail. "Garlin," I said to him with the catalog in front of me, "let me know your first, second and third choice for your Saturday DAPCEP classes this year."

Garlin took the catalog and considered his options. "Mama, there's nothing in here I want to take."

78

I stared at him. Nicely. Later, I filled out the application on his behalf and selected "Introduction to Chemistry" as his first choice.

When the acceptance letter came, Garlin acted surprised.

"Wait a minute, I thought we weren't going to pick anything this year."

I didn't have to think long about my answer. "I offered you an opportunity to participate in this decision, but you declined. Rest assured, you are not going to stay home and do *nothing*. So you can participate in the catalog selection process and pick a class of your choice or not, but you are going to take a class. And I am more than capable of making a selection for you."

After that, we never had that kind of discussion ever again. When the DAPCEP catalog came in the mail, he always gave me an A, B, and/or C choice after that.

My, my, my. Mission Accomplished.

The children might all be griping to their parents about all this "extra learning," but when they actually get to these academic enrichment courses on Saturdays, they have an opportunity to connect with old and new friends, plus do the work successfully and gain a sense of accomplishment and confidence that they can take from the school into the broader community. Success breeds success, the positive peer pressure was great, and what better way for your child to meet other kids whose parents have the same commitment and sense of sacrifice for their own children that you do?

I had another motive as well. Garlin was at a school where he was the only African American child in many of his classes. DAPCEP was in Detroit, and so his participation meant that he would interact with other African American students there, as well as with other young people of various ethnicities (Hispanic, Caucasian, Arab, Indian, etc.).

In the African American community, we have a term for this: "bi-lingual." It means that our children are able to comfortably relate to individuals of diverse socio-economic and cultural classes and races. This has, in the past, been especially important to African Americans, who have had to navigate multiple worlds in order to be successful. But it's really becoming a necessity for all young people; after all, our world as we know it is now global, and our children will need broad cultural competencies to compete successfully.

So Garlin participated in educational and sports activities that were either predominantly African American, predominantly Caucasian, or a mixture of numerous ethnicities, and he was exposed to international groups as well. When he got to the University of Michigan, when he did his internships, and when he ventured out into his profession as an engineer for Microsoft, he had been exposed to individuals from virtually every ethnicity with whom he would ultimately interact very comfortably.

And most importantly, he was conversant with his own African American heritage. This is critical. You must take your child to visit the institutions of your ethnic group—the museums, the religious organizations, the activities and events—that serve to ground your child and give them the confidence they need to venture out secure in their own worth, heritage and history.

It has served him well.

As an African American male, growing up in a predominately Caucasian environment, it was VERY important to my husband and me that Garlin knew who he was ethnically and that he be comfortable in his own skin. To achieve this goal, we had a lot of things going in our favor. We were blessed to be a part of multiple environments or peer groups that helped us show our son who his community was and allowed him the first hand opportunities to interact with and engage that community. First of all, both sets of grandparents lived in Detroit. In his early years, he spent five to six days out of seven in the neighborhoods in which Garlin Sr. and I grew up. This meant that he made friends, and interacted with many of the very same families that his parents had grown up with. Generational and institutional wisdom, experiences, and values were passed along openly and freely to our son in this close knit and family environment.

Secondly, our church (in which our family was and remains very active), Tabernacle Missionary Baptist, was located in the heart of Detroit. Foundational spiritual truths were learned and lived within the loving and nurturing environment of our family's faith and our faith family members.

Third, DAPCEP was located in Detroit. This was the place where Garlin could interact with other primarily African American students who looked like him, shared the same core educational values as he did and were just as smart as or smarter than he was. Many of these children became his close, lifelong friends. I'll discuss this critical aspect shortly.

And then finally, there was the Detroit Athletic Community. The sport in which Garlin was the most involved with was basketball. For many years, he participated on a variety of Detroit recreational, league and travel basketball teams. These teams were invaluable in teaching our son how to interact and be comfortable with other African American children of various social, economic, and cultural backgrounds. Our son's basketball teams played in places from the Detroit Police Athletic League Gymnasium to the mountaintop splendor of Salt Lake City, Utah, where he played as part of the Amateur Athletic Union (AAU).

Getting to Know You...

In middle school, you now have a new primary social network: your child's friend's parents. You'd be surprised at how much you can learn from them. Your child's friend may tell them something about your child that you might never otherwise know—good or bad. I know of one father whose son's best friend told his dad that their social group had made a pact not to put anything in their bodies that was toxic—specifically, drugs. This son was in a phase where he wasn't talking much to either parent, and so it was quite reassuring to know that their son had chosen some strong, positive friends. Had they not made that social connection, these parents would never have known this wonderful news about a very important personal decision their son had made.

Through these parent-friends, you can find out what's going on and who's doing what. Among other things, it's a great social pipeline for gaining advice about which schools to attend, which teachers to seek or avoid, in which programs to participate, and which places to allow or disallow your son or daughter to visit

For example, I was given advice about a particular teacher to avoid at school because she was supposed to have been really tough on the kids, requiring them to write several term papers during the course of the school year. "Oh you don't want Mrs. Smith—she makes them do the term papers, and gives too much homework." Hearing that salient advice and considering the source, I went straight to Mrs. Smith and said, "Please sign Garlin up for your class!"

You can also learn from parents with prior experience, those who have had older children go through the school and can offer perspective and history. As it turned out, Garlin had nine boys in our subdivision that were his same age and grade level, so I had nine mothers I could, and did, befriend! We became den mothers for Cub and Boy Scout troops, automatic carpool drivers and provided safe places for our sons to play.

You never know what benefits might accrue to you and your family as a result of making these connections. One piece of information can be the glue that pulls everything together. And the help that you offer will come back to you in the most unexpected of ways.

"Give and it shall be given onto you pressed down, shaken together and running over shall men give into your bosom."

~Luke 6:38 (KJV)

It worked for me. When we signed Garlin up for AAU (the gold standard of sports competition for young people all over the world), I was the "supermom" who handled the business of our AAU team. I typed contact directories of the team members, handled league and tournament registrations, posted practice/game schedules, and kept all rosters and records. I did ALL of the paperwork. And this was the pre-computer age! "I have amazing administrative skills," I told the coach. "If you handle training Garlin, I'll handle the books." I'm not bragging, but I was a coach's dream! Whenever he needed something done for the team administratively, he would call me, and it would be done!

I still have those records today.

A very dear friend of mine met once with a fitness trainer and it turned out that he was one of Garlin's fellow basketball players in AAU. She was just talking about her friend Yvonne, and the trainer interrupted her and asked: "Does she have a son named Garlin? I remember her; she was the team mom! Imagine my friend's surprise! He eventually became my trainer as well.

You just never know…

So join the parent groups. Offer to lead the Parent-Teacher Association, and have meetings at your home. Talk to parents at church, at neighborhood association meetings, or block clubs. Offer information to other parents as well. We are living in a very disconnected world where individualism reigns. The more connections we can make with others in our child's world, the better.

Promoting Your Child—It Comes From You!

The summer of his 8th grade year, Garlin went to an engineering program at the University of Michigan. Children competed from all over the country to get into that program. When Garlin got in, I called up the local newspaper and they did two articles, the first when he was accepted and the second when he completed the program with his various awards. Local newspaper people LOVE ready-to-run stories to fill content holes in the paper; sometimes all they need is a little push with a "good news" story. It's good to build a positive and productive relationship with the folks at your local newspaper, so that's just what I did! I would write the articles, include the pictures, highlight the main points, put my article into an envelope, and walk it to the newspaper. Eventually, the folks from the news desk would call me asking, "What is Garlin doing?" And of course, I'd answer in full detail.

"His AAU team is playing in the state tournament." Or, "He just received a volunteer service award from our church."

Whenever Garlin's team played in tournaments, for example, I'd call in every night to give them his basketball team scores, and I would give them the stats of all the other players as well as Garlin's. Then, I'd send pictures taken at the events. So guess what they had in the next edition on the sports page? I would say, "The team won game two of the state championship," and that headline or something close to it would appear in the newspaper. Having your child's name and/or picture show up in the newspaper is a really great thing. Your heart beats a little stronger because you are so proud, of course, but that's not the only reason. These articles also serve as independent documentation of your child's activities and accomplishments.

I was very careful to keep multiple copies of each and every one of Garlin's newspaper or magazine articles. Whenever I received a reporter's call, I would be ready. If email had been prevalent when Garlin was in high school, I would have been dangerous!

My trade secret? Communication, communication, communication! As parents, we are in the self-esteem-building business. We want to build up our children so that they can withstand the bricks and hard knocks of life, both above and below the belt. If you don't stand them up strong and straight, they'll blow with every wind. Our children do not get strong by themselves; you have to teach strength, model it, and then build it. If you can't write the article, let them write it! Ask their teacher or counselor help you write it! Ask a neighbor or relative to help you write it! Don't be afraid to ask for help. If your children know that they're successful, that success feeds upon itself. It motivates the child to do a little more or try a little harder or stick with that task a little bit longer because, in the end, they have learned in their heart of hearts that they can do it, and that knowledge leads to bigger and better things. Right?

To sum up: this is work. There is no way around it. And in a world that's moving much, much faster than we could have ever imagined when we were young, your child needs every single advantage that your wisdom and knowledge and vision can provide.

I'm sure you'll agree that your child is worth it.

MIDDLE SCHOOL: A SUMMARY OF CRITICAL TASKS

Preparation Strategies

❖ Make yourself known to your child's teachers and coaches, if applicable. Continue to be present at events and parent-teacher conferences; engage with them.

❖ Build a bank of goodwill with the school staff and teach your child to do the same thing. Favor is worth its weight in gold.

❖ Every day, ask what happened at school; use those open-ended conversations as a jumping off point for suggestions and recommendations. This is your opportunity as a parent to share your perspectives and your goals or values with your child, and to teach them what is right and what is wrong in their thinking and in their actions.

❖ Review your child's curriculum regularly and support your child's teacher in any way that you can.

❖ Seek opportunities for your child, internal or external to the school.

❖ Continue to set good expectations for your child; and watch them soar!

Partnering With Your Child's Educator

❖ Be sure to stay involved with your child at school. You may not realize it, but your presence is still necessary. Your child may know about latchkey, and taking the bus or walking to school independently, but they still need you there.

❖ It remains critical that you know your child's teachers and that they know you. Let them know that they can feel free to contact you if they have concerns about your child; and that you are available for assistance for field trips, or to provide auxiliary supplies, or participate in a reading hour.

❖ Show appreciation to your child's teachers for what they do well. There is nothing like receiving a note on a great project, or another activity that went above and beyond the average.

❖ Stay informed about the many opportunities at the school for your child outside of the formal classroom. If your child can write, and there's a school paper, encourage them to write for it. If they like music and there is a band, sign them up. If they are dramatic, encourage them to participate in school plays. Be on the lookout; and remember, you can only see opportunities if you're there—at the parent teacher conferences, the local school community organizations or the Parent Teachers Association, you'll be able to remain up-to-date.

CHAPTER 6

The High School Years: Keeping Them Motivated

The wisest parents have a way of motivating their children. I know one mother who, every year, was able to convince her child that this was THE most critical year of their educational lives. She was a lifelong educator and school counselor, so she was very effective at "making the case."

In the 1st grade, it was: "This year is so important. You're out of Kindergarten now, and you will start to get grades. Those grades count, and you're going to learn so much this year!"

In the 6th grade, it was: "This is your last year of elementary school. Your year here will set the foundation for junior high. Do well now, and you'll have a much easier time."

By the 9th grade, it was a different argument altogether: "This is the beginning of grades that count for college. They don't look at your 6th grade GPA; they start at the 9th grade. So now everything you do will determine where you will be able to go to college."

So, your child is now entering 9th grade. Or maybe they're further into their high school years. Wherever they are, there are some things particular to the high school experience that you should know.

What About the Child Who Is Struggling?

Get them help immediately! Don't wait, and don't take no for an answer.

For our family, Calculus was the bugaboo, and it didn't happen until Garlin's senior year. This was the first class that did not come easily to Garlin, and it presented his first significant high school challenge. His teacher wasn't exactly warm and fuzzy; you may find that even more when your child gets to high school. Don't think of this as a bad thing; it is actually quite useful in preparing the children for life beyond high school and to help them in their maturation process.

Having seen his first few homework assignments and tests, I mentioned to Garlin, "You seem to have a bit of a challenge here. We need to address this."

"Mom, I just didn't understand some of the homework this time."

"I understand. We should see about getting you some extra help. Does your teacher have office hours?"

Garlin answered, "Yes."

"What time?"

It turned out that the math teacher's office hours were at 6:30 a.m. He wasn't exactly overjoyed at the prospect of attending these office hours on a regular basis. Who could blame him? But this was an opportunity to show him that life was about making the best of a bad situation.

"That's okay," I told Garlin. "This is a tough subject and you have a tough teacher, but he's just trying to help the kids prepare for college. Life is about facing challenges squarely in the face and then doing something to overcome them. You are going to have to start going to meet with your teacher during his posted office hours. This is your opportunity to get the extra help that you need. You will be able to review your homework assignments and ask any other questions that will help you understand the concepts better and solve the equations correctly. Given the early hour of day for office hours, I suspect that you will have the opportunity to receive quite a bit of one-on-one assistance from your teacher."

I went on to explain that there was no shame in not grasping these Calculus concepts instantaneously. Everybody needs a little extra help at some point, and most of us need a lot of help. This situation would turn into something truly tragic if he or we as a family failed to recognize what was going on and then failed to get help.

I wanted to encourage my son to show him that this was a problem that, with a little extra effort and initiative on his part, could be solved. I went on to explain how going to these early morning office hours would help him. I explained that this would facilitate him getting to know his teacher better, learning what his expectations were, and how he managed his classroom and coursework. I also explained that this was a golden opportunity for his teacher to get to know him better. The teacher would see up close and personally how Garlin's mind was working, when he was on the right track, and when he veered off onto the wrong track. I also told him that I believed that, by forming a more personal and positive relationship with his teacher, he would garner favor. By attending those early morning office hours, his teacher would be able to see that he was extremely serious about his school work and especially the Calculus course. Then, his teacher would be able to learn firsthand exactly how Garlin was processing the information presented to him. When Garlin was processing the information correctly, he could be encouraged. When he veered off the mark, he could be steered safely back on course and be even more encouraged because he would be learning from his mistakes. Then last but certainly not least, I suggested to Garlin that, because of his faithfulness in working with his teacher, when the exams, quizzes, or even homework assignments were turned in, he would potentially gain the benefit of those last vestiges of favor and get credit for the portions of his work that he performed correctly, even if the final answer was incorrect. Why was that? Because in showing his work, the teacher would clearly see where Garlin was on the right track and then where he veered off. He would at least get some points for the problem, versus getting the whole problem wrong!

With that strategy in mind, Garlin marched up to his Calculus teacher's office hours faithfully day after day, week after week. He was able to quickly turn 'not-knowing' into confident 'knowing' and that was certainly a much more comfortable place for my child. Sometimes, they would only meet for five or ten minutes. At other times, they would meet for the full hour. At different points in his studies, he could relax and come to office hours two or three mornings a week versus four or five, depending upon how he was doing in the course work. I was trying to teach Garlin that he was to stick with this process whether he was doing good or needed a little extra assistance. The success was in staying on top of things, rather than employing a hit-or-miss work ethic.

So, at the end of the semester, Garlin's teacher felt good about Garlin, and the feeling was mutual. Garlin came to have a much closer relationship with his teacher because he demonstrated seriousness as a student. After a full year with this instructor, Garlin had aced his Calculus course both semesters and his instructor wrote him a wonderful letter of recommendation for college. See the next page for the letter:

FARMINGTON HIGH SCHOOL

Dear Sir/Madam,   October 27, 1999

My name is Brian Shaw; I am a mathematics and engineering teacher at Farmington High School. I am writing in regards to Garlin Gilchrist and his qualifications to be a representative at the AMHPS Symposium. Garlin was a student in my Principles of Engineering class, Honors PreCalculus class, and is currently in my Introduction to Calculus class. I have also witnessed his interactions with other adults and his peers in extra-curricular activities.

Garlin's academic abilities are far above average. He receives high marks in my classes consistently throughout the year, which is a significant achievement. He is a successful student in classes that are very demanding, competitive, and graded with strict parameters. I would classify him in the 90th percentile of all my students. His academic ability is complimented by his work ethic. Garlin's commitment to his education is unquestionable, he is a self-motivated student. He strives to fully understand conceptual topics, and their applications, not just learn the methodology. Garlin is willing to give additional effort if necessary to succeed. He pursues my help outside of class in order to get further instruction and assistance if necessary, in addition to his personal study time.

Garlin's social skills are also excellent. In the classroom, he is respectful to authority while maintaining a pleasant and humorous atmosphere. He is not afraid to ask thoughtful questions, and often shares insightful ideas. Furthermore, he works well with his classmates. He is willing to assist others as well as receive assistance from his peers; he is cooperative and helpful. This outstanding ability to interact with his peers as well as authority is one of the main reasons I recommend him as a representative. Garlin is also a very well rounded student. Outside of the classroom, he is involved in numerous activities including varsity basketball. He is a dedicated and successful player, yet his primary focus remains on education. His excellent balance of athletics and academics displays his organizational skills and self-discipline. His classmates and other teachers also think very highly of him. His social abilities are diverse and impressive.

Overall, I highly recommend Garlin to you. I believe that he would be an excellent representative at the AMHPS Symposium. I know Garlin has been an award-winning participant at other academic programs (SCEEP at University of Michigan) and I believe that participation in your symposium would be mutually beneficial.

Sincerely,

Brian Shaw

NCA
Accredited by the
North Central Association of
Colleges and Schools

Farmington
PUBLIC SCHOOLS

32000 SHIAWASSEE   FARMINGTON, MICHIGAN 48336-3261   (248) 189-3455   Fax (248) 089-3474

I was pleased with this experience. It set up some very important principles that we were able to employ in college:

- Get help at the FIRST signs of distress, not when the boat has sunk.

- Relationships matter. Go to your professor's office hours; get to know them and allow them to get to know you. You never know when something even beyond your grade for that particular class will be at stake.

- Be and remain open with your family—they can be a second or third set of eyes or ears to spot potential problem areas and help work through your options.

Later, when Garlin got to college and struggled in a class, I would remind him: "Garlin, we're having a 'Mr. Brian moment' here." He knew exactly what I was talking about, and it served to be a great trigger for him to get back on track by leaving his emotions out of it!

Getting to Know You

At this point, just as important as getting to know your child's teachers is getting to know your child's counselor. They have the latest information on colleges, on extracurricular and enrichment programs locally as well as nationwide, and they know how to help get your child ready and engaged. By his senior year, I made it a point to see Garlin's counselor at least once a month, to see what new information I might obtain.

In the beginning of your child's high school career, you should focus with the counselor on your child's course schedule and compare their course progression with a list of likely colleges to which they will apply. Backtrack from the 12th grade to extrapolate what they will need to take first in every subject. This will include languages and language arts, mathematics, physical and social sciences, etc. If your child is having disciplinary problems, the counselor will be a very close associate. In either event, make sure that you know them and that they know you and your child. The counselor should know that you want your child to go to college, and that you are certainly very much interested in the scholarships and/or grants that they may be able to secure!

It should go without saying that you should attend every single parent-teacher conference. That should not even be a question in your mind. You may not be able trust your child to tell you everything that is going on in school. Even if they are doing well, you will usually receive valuable and insightful information from the teacher about what more you might be able to do as a parent, or nuances of your child's behavior that need to be addressed, or an array of other valuable information and tidbits about your child and his/her education.

Taking "Benefit of the Doubt" To a New Level

In church, we call it "grace." In school, we call it "benefit of the doubt."

You heard me mention it in the last chapter. I said that it would happen as your child—and you as parents—make your presence known at school in a positive fashion. Now, you need to teach your child something else: that high school is good practice for college, because it is here that your child may first experience teaching that is not "spoon-fed." In other words, your child will have to process a lot of the information himself, and take a lot of non-classroom time to figure out what they have just been taught. No longer is your child sitting like an obedient, eager bird in the nest with its mouth open, ready for the mama bird to place the worm in it. Instead, they are interacting with the material, doing their own original research, and learning how to have a true exchange with their teachers and peers. It can be very exciting, but only if your child explicitly understands that they have to make that transition.

How to Get the Benefit of the Doubt

Here's the principle: Benefit of the doubt comes through a proven track record of effort. If your child turns in a math assignment with little work in the margins and all wrong answers, that's a pretty good indicator that they didn't work through very much of the material. If they go up to their teacher and say, "I didn't understand the assignment," that simply will not do; by that time, it's a little late for that kind of response.

Here's how you as a parent might counsel them. If it is, for example, a math course, say something like this:

"Go to your room and write down everything that you know to do on every problem based on what you've already learned."

One of two things will happen:

99

Option 1: They'll go in their room and sulk at the four walls and wonder how long they can reasonably stay in there until you back down or let them come out, or:

Option 2: They'll find out they know more than they thought, get halfway through some problems, and can now pinpoint exactly where they are stuck. The fog begins to clear; and as the fog clears, the frustration begins to diminish.

If they follow Option 1, you have a lot more work to do. You have to meet with the teacher and your child and painstakingly map out a plan for them to get the help they need. It may be that your child should return to a lower math level first, in order to establish a better foundation. They may need tutoring, additional practice problems, or more hands-on review with the teacher. If that's the case, it's okay. No shame there; making academic adjustments is NOT tantamount to failure. You as a parent need to be open to making these kinds of adjustments in the best interests of your child. You're just doing what you need to do to make sure your child is successful.

If, however, they follow Option 2, you're on your way! Your child gains confidence when they find that personal effort results in visible success. They discover that they know more than they thought they did, and they realize that they don't have to be frustrated. With that increase in confidence, they are better able to admit what they don't understand and are more likely to seek help. As a result, your child's teacher is impressed that their student has worked to the limit of their capacity, and that they have put forth a good effort. The teacher then becomes a co-advocate with you in the education of your child; they see that the child is trying, and therefore are willing and available so that your child can be successful in that class. You now have the teacher on your child's side; in fact, they have now become a fan!

Now that the teacher is an advocate in the student's learning, your child is now in a position to be on the receiving end of this elusive thing called "benefit of the doubt." "I know that Johnny understood this concept during our review," they might say when reviewing a test or homework. "It looks like he just added wrong. Instead of 10 points, I'll just take 4 points off." That could be the difference between a C and a B, or a B versus an A.

You may find that you have to go through this process more than just once. Hopefully, after 9th or 10th grade, the process will become ingrained as a habit in your child, and they will grow in their ability to absorb and interact with the material, identify their weak spots without becoming discouraged or frustrated, and communicate effectively and openly those deficiencies with their teachers. These are all critical skills for them to take to college.

Parents, you can contribute to your child's ability to receive benefit of the doubt as well. If you are an involved, respectful, and contributing parent, your child is more likely to be chosen by the school staff for academic programs, financial awards, newspaper profiles, special travel opportunities, and the like. You never know what those opportunities might be!

Building Up the Portfolio

You'll hear more about this later, but the key tool for promoting your child's success is their personal portfolio. We've talked a lot about academics, and academics is certainly the first item to capture the attention of college and scholarship decision makers. But there are two other aspects of your child's development that are absolutely necessary to ensuring their competitiveness and positioning them for success. These are community service and leadership.

Community Service

College selection boards, scholarship selection boards, and admissions offices are asking this question of young applicants: "What are you giving back?" As parents, you have to help figure out how to create community service opportunities. For example, we knew an elementary school counselor who knew that Garlin was good with computers and basketball, so she asked him to create an after-school computer lab at her school. She was happy with his work, and as she observed how he interacted with the children, she also asked him to organize an after-school basketball league. The kids loved playing basketball and they loved him! So that was one great opportunity for community service that turned into two. It was a way for him to give back, a way for the school to benefit, and a way for me to document Garlin's community service activities.

There were other opportunities as well. I approached the Detroit Urban League, the National Association for the Advancement of Colored People (NAACP), the Optimist Club and other organizations and found many, many things for Garlin to do. Our local chapter of the Urban League has a program called the College Club, where students who joined the Urban League would have an opportunity to engage in community service and benefit as area colleges came to facilitate on-site college admissions applications. Local and national chapters also offered various scholarships.

With the NAACP, Garlin became a junior member, attended youth meetings, and participated in various community projects. With the police department, for example, there was the neighborhood watch, and working booths during various neighborhood events. Garlin manned one of the booths, etching identification information on bicycles or attending to a carnival ride or game. Essentially, he made himself available to do whatever the officers or community event organizers wanted him to do.

Parents, here is some homework for you: Find those kinds of organizations in your community that provide such opportunities. Start with the local chapters of national organizations such as the Lions Club, the Optimist Club, Kiwanis, the Humane Society, the NAACP, and the Urban League. Make sure you start early in your child's high school career and provide plenty of outlets for them to serve.

When you locate and place your child in these activities, make sure you get documentation. Not every group in which your child participates realizes the importance of these youth portfolios, and sometimes we have to help them. Garlin was working with the local police department on a bicycle safety project. I needed a community service certificate for his portfolio, and they didn't have them. That didn't stop me. First, I explained the need for a certificate of participation to the event leader. Then, after ascertaining that there was no community service/documentation, I asked if I could assist by creating a draft certificate subject to their official approval that could be distributed to the children. Once I received their approval, I created the certificate, not just for Garlin, but for all of the young people working at the particular event. I asked for the logo, the proper names of the officials involved, the correct individual(s) to place on the signature line...and I didn't mind being the secretary. I'd buy ready-made certificates, type in the names, get the appropriate signatures, and lo and behold, Garlin and his fellow teens had great documentation of all the good things they were doing. Generally, the leaders would be very pleased because this was an aspect of planning the community event that they had not previously thought of. They were happy to show their appreciation for the children's service, especially given that they received no monetary remuneration. Even more often, the parents of the other volunteering children would thank me for providing their children with such documentation.

Leadership

Leadership is important. If you want to document that your child is a leader, you have to help them develop and then document their acquired leadership skills. Leaders are probably born, not made; but even born leaders need help honing their skills. Secondly, every human being is called to lead something—a group at work or in an organization, one other person as a mentor, a family, or a particular subject matter...you get the idea. Where do leadership skills come from? How can you tap into potential areas of leadership development for your child?

Start with listening to others. No one person knows everything or has done everything. Therefore, we need each other. That old adage, "It takes a village to raise a child," is an old adage for a reason. Talk to people. Ask questions. Find out what worked and what didn't work for others. That's wisdom.

Again I repeat: our children do not come with an instruction manual on how to raise them. We must learn from both our experiences and the collective wisdom of others to help guide us and show us the path to success. The path will be different for each person.

Continue by listening to your child. Parents, understand that each child in your household will differ in their temperament, in their desires and in their skills and abilities. It is our job as parents to look for and pay close attention to and to note the 'bent' or 'direction' God has outlined for each child, individually. There is no one size fits all scenario. One child may like to work with his hands. Another may be musically or artistically inclined. Yet another may be gifted in math, science or engineering. The technical things just click for her. The last may be intellectually stimulated through books and writings, and be creative in this fashion. The bottom line is that the possibilities are endless.

Pay attention to the God-given gifts and talents that are deposited into your child; these speak to possible areas of leadership. Pay attention to what other people around you are doing. Read the newspapers, research the web, and talk to people. When you go to weddings, graduations, barbeques, family reunions, and other social or business events, don't talk just about the weather; ask, "What are you doing? What are your children doing?" You just might stumble onto something you can use for your child, or even yourself.

It worked that way for me. Through talking with another parent at a social event, I found out about a program designed for future leaders called the "Presidential Classroom" (www.presidentialclassroom.org). Remember the iconic picture of former President Bill Clinton as a teenager shaking hands with our late President, John F. Kennedy? Clinton was in the 1960 inaugural class of that very program started by President Kennedy himself. There is a virtual "Who's Who" list of leaders who participated in that program as teenagers. We signed Garlin up and he went to Washington for ten days in February 1999. It just so happened that this visit coincided with the presidential impeachment of President William Jefferson Clinton. Talk about an exciting time! This group of young future leaders visited the Supreme Court and other historical sites, and debated a bill on the floor of the House of Representatives and Senate. Each student had the opportunity to interact with at least one of their federal legislators. More than four-hundred thirty five students from all over the country formed a mock House of Representatives and Senate, and coalesced into caucuses to model how legislation is formulated, debated and enacted into law.

"Mom, there are about 390 members of one political party here," Garlin told me. That was great for him; as one of few members of the opposite political party, he was able to receive significant debate time and great debate training. He was even able to make a two-minute speech on the House floor! It was thrilling. And ironically, the theme topic was Ethics in Politics. The students even appeared on C-SPAN.

What was particularly exciting to me about all of this was the fact that twenty-five years earlier I had received an opportunity to do something very similar. My high school government teacher called me out of class one day and told me to sit down right then and write a 500-word essay about what I thought I would gain by going to Washington, D.C. to see my government in action. The sponsoring group picked two winning essays from each state in the Union to form a "mock Senate" and then sent the winners to Washington D.C. for ten days. I was thrilled to be selected as one of the winners from the State of Michigan! This was my very first time being away from home without my family. I was blessed to fly on an airline for the very first time in my life, and it was my first time staying on a college campus. We were housed in dorms at a local Washington D.C.-area college. I had breakfast with Senator Carl Levin and lunch and dinner with then-U.S. Congresswoman Martha Griffith. My experience, as an impressionable 17-year-old high school senior, was eerily parallel to Garlin's, as my visit was one month before the late President Richard Nixon resigned from office.

But I digress. Garlin's minority political status allowed him to have the opportunity to stand out as a debater, and so next year when asked, his Presidential Classroom Program

Director was happy to write a wonderful letter of recommendation. We were able to use that letter for a number of other scholarship and leadership programs, including a great community service initiative called Inroads, as well as for Who's Who in America for High School Students.

These kinds of experiences allow your child to exercise and demonstrate leadership. And just as you did with your community service documentation, make sure to document your child's leadership activities. It's great for those college applications, definitely, but even greater for life.

HIGH SCHOOL:
A SUMMARY OF CRITICAL TASKS

Preparation Strategies

❖ Engage with your child's counselor, to get a sense of what you need to be doing at each grade level to prepare them for college and find out what other activities—both academic and non-academic—are available for your child.

❖ Continue to ask what happened at school, but have reasonable expectations. Your child might not be completely forthcoming at all times! You need to find out some things for yourself.

❖ Begin researching colleges in 9th grade. Look at potential schools online with your child and make plans, if possible, to visit some of them during spring break in the summer months. Take advantage of college tours sponsored by schools, community organizations, or churches, where your child can see firsthand a number of different schools at one time and make comparisons. Make sure that your child has completed, or is on track to complete, the course work and preparation required for the schools in which they are most interested.

❖ Make sure that your child has ample opportunities for volunteering and leadership activities. Help them to understand that the universe does not revolve around them and they have a responsibility to give of themselves to others.

❖ Provide as much opportunity as possible for your child to get training in test-taking skills, especially for the ACT and SAT. They'll need the practice for the junior and senior year especially, when they will have to take the standardized tests that determine their college direction and options.

❖ Work with your child's counselor to ensure that your child has taken all requisite courses to graduate, and the requisite standardized college admission tests, including the ACT and the SAT.

❖ Don't be shy! Speak up, without bragging, to share your child's accomplishments with the media! Did they win a school award? Send it to the local/community newspaper. Did they get Employee of the Month as a part-timer at CVS? Let people know! Newspapers are looking for good news items to fill space, and yours is a personal interest story that they often will be quick to tell; even if you have to be the one to tell it. The bonus is that these articles will become a part of your child's winning portfolio, which we will discuss in more detail later.

Partnering With Your Child's Educator

The best thing to do with your child's educator is to arm them with *information*. No one educator or one school can keep up with the plethora of information now available on websites, in organizations and in libraries.

Secondly, make the educator's job easy. If there are scholarship applications and packages to be sent, make sure the information is filled out accurately and completely. Make it very clear where school officials are to sign, what documents need to be included in your packet, and exactly what the filing deadlines are. Make copies of everything, just in case something gets lost. Provide stamps or other postage if necessary; it gives your counselor one less thing to coordinate on behalf of your child.

CHAPTER 7

The Senior Year: Your Full Time Job!

"**Y**vonne, we want you to enter Garlin for the National Society of Black Engineers Golden Torch Award (NSBE GTA) for Male High School Engineering Students."

At the beginning of Garlin's senior year, we received a call from the DAPCEP High School Administrator, Margaret Tucker. She was calling me in the third year that this prestigious award was being issued. Our son, now a high school senior, had six years of DAPCEP participation under his belt, and needless to say, I was excited by her call.

For the first two years of its inception, the NSBE GTA for Female High School Engineering Student of the Year had been granted to two young women from Detroit, both of whom had been participants in DAPCEP. Ms. Tucker saw this as a possible obstacle for Garlin. "We don't think another DAPCEP student can win this prestigious national award for a third time in a row," she said, "but we want you to go ahead and apply anyway."

Don't we all have that notion that our child is the best? If you don't, nobody else will. As a blues great once said, "If your mama don't love you, don't nobody love you!"

"Not a problem," I responded to Ms. Tucker's invitation. "Who won in years past is none of my business," I told her. "Just let me pull something together."

Margaret then gave me the zinger: "We need Garlin's application in less than two weeks."

She had thrown down the gauntlet.

The application required an official transcript, test scores, three letters of recommendation, and a picture. That's all that was required.

How could I portray my son in the best possible light? He had done the consistent hard work to get to the point where DAPCEP saw fit to nominate him. He had made the grades in school and done the countless volunteer hours. Working in conjunction with the school, the church, and the community, his dad and I had positioned him well for the future.

I knew that nobody could champion him more than I could as his mother. Others may encounter our children, love our children, but they can only help so much. It is incumbent upon you as the parent to roll up your sleeves and make sure that the world knows what you already know. I can't say it enough: YOU are your child's greatest advocate!

And so, I began the arduous task of putting together a portfolio that ultimately resulted in Garlin's receiving this prestigious award. The entire process was made easier because I had been organizing my son's activities, awards, and significant information for many years. I had a special section carved out in our home where I kept important documents that chronicled Garlin's accomplishments and growth.

I gave them more than they asked for. I gave them a knockout Portfolio.

A few days before Christmas, we received a phone call. It was the NSBE GTA Selection Committee. "Mrs. Gilchrist, this is the NSBE Selection Board for the GTA. Your son, Garlin, has been selected and we want you to know that his application is the finest we've ever seen. You have set the new standard for applications!"

On March 24, 2000, Garlin received the most prestigious award of his young life: The NSBE Golden Torch Award as the Male High School Engineering Student of the Year: a national award for the most promising male high school student who was interested in engineering.

What was in that application? I'm glad you asked! I virtually compiled Garlin's entire high school career into distinct categories that I will explain fully in this chapter.

> **Categories in the Winning NSBE Portfolio for the Golden Touch Award (GTA):**
>
> - **NSBE GTA ESSAY**
>
> - **RESUME**
>
> - **ACADEMICS**
>
> - **COMMUNITY SERVICE**
>
> - **LEADERSHIP**
>
> - **ATHLETICS**
>
> - **WORK EXPERIENCE**
>
> - **RECOMMENDATIONS**
>
> - **PHOTOGRAPHS**

The package began with an essay: "Why do I think I deserve this award?" The first thing I did was to have Garlin write that one-page essay. I had Garlin write it himself. I DID NOT WRITE THE ESSAY FOR HIM. I strongly believe that a student must do his or her own work. You can proof it, but not write it. If he could not explain in his own words why he was worthy, then he did not deserve to get the award, right? My job was to be his sounding board if he asked. He did not.

Then, I worked with him to develop a resume, a summary of what he had done and accomplished thus far in his life. Because we kept excellent records, we had everything we needed: all of the courses he had taken both at school and while attending extracurricular academic programs, detail of the volunteer activities in which he had been involved over the years, sports accomplishments, academic honors, special acquired skills, and enrichment experiences such as travel, etc. We also listed the classes in which he was currently enrolled, as it was too soon for them to show up on his transcript.

The next section was devoted to academics. We asked for letters of recommendation from Garlin's principal and the president of our local school board. All of those years of being a very involved parent was now about to bear fruit. I knew the school board superintendent personally and felt comfortable making the call to request a letter. Garlin graduated from high school with a 3.96 GPA, and we felt confident that his academic section was indeed very strong.

Next was community service. Garlin had worked faithfully with his father and on his own in our church essentially all of his life. He participated in the Sunday Church School and the Optimist Club. He worked with his dad in the Bus Ministry, and the "Never Alone - Sick and Shut in Bible Study" with me, just to name a few things. Garlin also tutored students at a local elementary school and as mentioned earlier, he had helped establish a computer lab and basketball team for the children at that elementary school. He participated in fundraisers and car washes to raise monies for basketball team tournament travel. He was always on the lookout for opportunities to render service to the elderly. I looked for things to keep his hands from being idle, without overwhelming him or cutting into his study time.

Next was leadership. This was a category for which I knew my son was not just well-suited, but exceptional. It was very easy for my husband and me to perceive a God-given gift of leadership in Garlin, and we truly wished to nurture that gifting. Programs such as Presidential Classroom, The Detroit Urban League, and DAPCEP helped to nurture Garlin's natural leadership skills. Garlin was named Who's Who Among High School Students every year of high school. The Presidential Classroom's Flagship Scholars Program in Washington, D.C. gave student leaders in their local communities the opportunity to view how the federal government works while developing personal, leadership, and diplomatic skills. The students did research, wrote reports to address major political issues, and debated those issues to drive consensus and to produce legislation for the mock House of Representatives.

Garlin also had a chance to serve as a radio talk show host for the program "Making It Happen." Every week, he was responsible for planning, organizing, and executing a live youth radio talk show in Detroit. He invited other students to be his guests, answered live telephone calls and served as the show's producer. The show covered topics that were of particular interest to other high school students and their parents as well. I was very proud of the way he handled himself and the show. Garlin also volunteered to lead various youth committees at our church.

Garlin had lots of items to include in the leadership category of his portfolio. But that was no accident. We made a conscious decision to groom Garlin for leadership. You must constantly be on the lookout for opportunities like this, and you must insist that your child serve in these capacities. It won't hurt them. Don't worry about them saying, "I don't want to do this," and pouting. You can enjoy their appreciation later; now is the time to parent.

The next section was athletics. His AAU coach wrote a letter of recommendation and we also included his varsity letters, awards, and copies of newspaper articles about his participation in basketball, track and field and other tournaments. In that section, we also included Garlin's *academic* letter, given to all athletes who maintained an overall GPA of 3.3 or better. What? Your school doesn't have academic letters? They seem to value the athlete more than the scholar? Then this is a great opportunity for you to advocate for your child as well as other children! Push for academic letters, and push your school system to celebrate academic achievement with the same vigor and excitement that they reserve for athletic prowess. It will make all the difference in the world. School culture is everything!

WORK EXPERIENCE

We also included Garlin's extensive work resume. That brings up another important point: Sometimes, finding out what a child does NOT want to do is just as important as them discovering what kind of work ignites their passion.

On my job, one of the departments that I managed was run by a very bright young man by the name of Antoine, who was in his mid-twenties and not very much older than Garlin. He was an expert in all phases of servicing computers and helped keep my division's desktops and laptops running smoothly.

One evening Antoine and I were working late on a major system overhaul and while talking I discovered that he owned and operated an independent computer company called "Three Wonders of Computers."

I knew that Antoine was a brilliant young man and the fact that he owned his own computer consulting company impressed me on many levels. I liked his independence, his entrepreneurial spirit, and I certainly appreciated his outstanding work ethic, outgoing personality and wit. Last but not least, I knew that Garlin was very interested in learning all he could about computers and I was hopeful that Antoine might be able to help cultivate that interest.

So I asked Antoine to tell me all about his company. The more I heard the more I liked what I was hearing.

"Antoine," I asked, "would you consider hiring my son to work for your company?"

"Mrs. Gilchrist, Three Wonders of Computers is a SMALL business and my partner and I don't have any employees. We solicit contracts and then execute them ourselves. Besides, we don't have any money to hire any employees."

"Who said anything about money?" I replied. A plan was already formulating in my mind, just that fast. "I'd like to make you an offer. Since your company builds and repair computers, I'd like to purchase a brand new computer from you. But there is one condition: My son, Garlin has to build it. Hire him, then teach him how to build my computer from scratch and we have a deal. I'm asking you to bring Garlin alongside you—teach him the things that you know about computer hardware and software."

And this was the deal-maker. I told him:

"But he will not need a salary. The knowledge and experience he will gain from working with you will FAR outweigh any per hour salary you could offer to pay him. If you would mentor my son and teach him half the things you know about computers, he would be overjoyed and his dad and I would thank and appreciate you forever."

Antoine grimaced. "Well, I'll have to think about your offer. Everything depends upon my opinion of your son and whether I believe he would be a suitable, potential employee."

"Fine," I said, "that sounds fair to me. I accept."

Antoine said, "I tell you what. I'd like to interview Garlin first then make my decision about/regarding your offer. If I like him, I'll hire him. But if not, I won't. I can't promise any more than that."

Then, he made one more request. "This is what I want for the price of one custom built computer. A good old-fashioned fried chicken dinner with lots of real french fries.

Do that for me, and I'll interview him for sure."

"Fair enough," I told him. I invited him to dinner at my home, and made arrangements for them to meet. They actually had a lot in common. Antoine played basketball in high school and college, was young and hip and they hit it off instantly. They ordered the supplies for the computer, and Antoine showed Garlin how to build it from the ground up. Garlin worked for Antoine for the next two years, and the experience was amazing, far exceeding my initial hopes and dreams. They built custom desktop and laptop computers, set up office networks and installed computer security systems all over town. In one of their larger orders Garlin was able to help build and install a computer security system for a major recreational facility in Detroit.

This was 1999; remember Y2K? Garlin had an opportunity to work on hardware and software solutions for that looming 'turn of the century' threat. It turned out to be not much of a threat, but the experience proved invaluable. It was during those two years that Garlin discovered he liked the software side of engineering but not the hardware side. That was good information to know as he was exploring various engineering career paths early in his high school days.

Antoine became a big brother to Garlin, teaching him a valuable skill, and helping him narrow down his computer engineering interests.

My approach to Antoine was intentional. I didn't need him to pay Garlin to work at his company. I needed him to transfer his smarts and know-how to Garlin. And I was willing to buy a computer for him, and fix 'real' french fries on a regular basis.....in order to ensure that Garlin had access to this valuable resource.

At the end of that second year, Antoine moved to California. He and Garlin remain friends to this day.

I have a second story about work. One day Garlin said out of the blue, "Mom I think I would like to do biomedical engineering. I want to make spare body parts and big buttons for 'old' people like you."

Kids will say anything.

After I patted him on top of the head, I put the word out. Not too long afterwards, I discovered that Kettering University sponsored a joint program with Wayne State University's (WSU) Minority High School Science Education Program. (MHSSEP) Garlin presented/shared his current knockout portfolio at the MHSSEP family interview and was accepted into the eight-week program.

Garlin was paired with a prominent WSU researcher who was conducting medical research on the effect of anti-depressant drugs on rodents. I certainly wouldn't be caught dead with a rodent, but Garlin thought the assignment was great! He did so well that this professor had him write an abstract of his internship and submit it to the American Medical Association. The abstract was accepted and Garlin was published! He then ended up participating in the American Minorities Health Professional Society Conference, a national event sponsored by a group of HBCUs (Historically Black Colleges and Universities).

Garlin was eventually selected to defend his research project in front of a group of medical school deans. He won the Grand Prize!

A few months later, he announced: "I really had a great summer and truly appreciate all the wonderful opportunities presented to me. But I really don't think I like biomedical engineering after all, Mom." I was unfazed. I understood this principle: the only way to discover what you want to do is to find ways to immerse yourself in that work. You will typically find out what you DON'T want to do first. But if you wait until you choose a major, graduate from college and get a job, you could be very, very disappointed and end up regretting your choice of profession. I definitely did not want this to happen to our son.

In the early days of your child's education, it's not about the money. It's about the experience and the exposure.

I wanted my son to have a 'career' not a 'job'. A passion, not just a paycheck. Fulfillment matters! And I was willing to help him find that path to success, period!

Remember the classic Thomas Edison story? When asked about his numerous failed attempts to harness electricity, he replied, "If I find 10,000 ways something won't work, I haven't failed. I am not discouraged, because every wrong attempt discarded is another step forward." The same applies here. Every time your child discovers something they don't like, they are one step closer to discovering their passion.

Finally, we had letters of recommendation. Three were required. Because we had been so active, and I had been diligent in getting Garlin's name and reputation out to the community, we were able to take our pick of recommendations; from the mayor and city council and congressional representative, to the educators in his extracurricular activities, to his coaches and mentors, and finally his teachers and even the school principal! I worked for GM and one of their senior engineers, Mr. Lewis Cole, Jr., mentored Garlin. Garlin passed out leaflets and helped campaign for political candidates, so we had that connection as well. I ended up asking for character references from a variety of persons—people who had known him since birth and all along the way. I also secured additional letters of recommendation from some notable individuals, including:

- Senator Carl Levin—it turned out that Garlin Sr.'s good friend and former classmate worked in the Senator's office, and was more than happy to intervene on our behalf with him.

- Derrick E. Scott—Director of the Multicultural Engineering Programs Office in the University of Michigan College of Engineering. He had, through his office's Summer Engineering Academy, been one of Garlin's most important mentors and supporters. Our son was in numerous programs at Michigan focused on activities to pique his interest in science, technology, engineering, and math (STEM) fields. The programs did exactly what they were designed to do, and Garlin was ultimately admitted to the University.

- The Late Rev. Frederick G. Sampson—Our beloved Pastor of Tabernacle Missionary Baptist Church, who had been named every year by *Ebony* magazine as one of the top ten Black preachers in America. Rev. Sampson wrote a glowing letter that I am sure helped put Garlin's application over the top!

Needless to say, we had a wonderful Christmas! NSBE sent the family to the award ceremony on March 24, 2000 in Charlotte, North Carolina. Garlin spoke in front of 5,000 people and I have never been more proud of my son than I was that evening. As a family we had focused heavily on communication when he was little ("Sit up straight, hold your head up, not down, speak up so that you can be heard, not just seen," et.al.), and so it was not foreign to him to march up to that podium and give his speech in front of students, educators, professionals, and CEOs.

The speech was so good that four or five CEOs made reference to it. When we attended the ceremonies the next year, they were still commenting about Garlin's speech!

The final three-ringed portfolio that I submitted on Garlin's behalf was one inch thick. It contained everything, from resumes to certificates and letters of recommendation, to local articles about Garlin. It was a portfolio whose preparation was years in the making. I had at least one binder for every school year. Once called upon to meet Garlin's destiny, every item, every piece of paper, was where it was supposed to be. My job became simply to compile that information and organize it into a readable, impressive package. Fortunately for us, that is exactly what happened!

The portfolio is a public document to showcase your child's accomplishments and "wow" whoever is viewing it...including your child. It is a great way to build self-esteem and get your child, and the whole family, involved in celebrating and reflecting on their successes and struggles. This is especially true for younger children, as they are involved in many different sorts of activities and are trying to find their way in the world at large. As the child grows older, and begins to focus on particular gifts and talents a bit more, the portfolio helps to tangibly record that journey and to confirm the progress made.

That wasn't all that Garlin won. In October of that same year, he received a confirmation of early acceptance from the University of Michigan. In order to receive an early acceptance from a college or university, you have to be aggressive. I was extremely aggressive when it came to my son's education. I did not wait until the last minute to do my research, and in doing so I found that there was something called an "early college acceptance." Your completed college admissions application had to be ready for submission earlier than most 12th grade students. This meant being ready with letters of recommendation, ready with the essays, ready with your child's official transcripts, and any other information requested on the college application. And, you had to have looked into these types of areas well in advance of the senior year, which, of course, I had done.

What are the benefits of applying and obtaining acceptance into a college or university early in your high school senior year? **Money!** Universities only have so much money to hand out and once they do, it's gone. So if your child doesn't apply to college until December or February or even later in some instances of their senior year, and the student gets accepted, they may qualify for academic or need-based aid but may not get it from the college of their choice because the college has simply run out of money. Since you clearly do not want that to happen to your child, then you should consider preparing your child to apply early!

By the 12th grade, I was seeing the counselor nearly every week. Every Monday, I sent Garlin to school with a large grey envelope. In that envelope were a number of scholarship application packages that we had processed during the previous week. Most of the time they required an official high school transcript, official ACT or SAT test scores, and a statistical profile about the school district in which Garlin's school was located. Often these organizations or schools also wanted a letter of recommendation (or two)—typically from the counselor, teacher, or principal.

Because we were applying for so many scholarships, I tried to make it as easy as possible for the school staff. I applied yellow signature "sticky-notes" to indicate where school signatures were required. I included in the grey envelope a checklist that allowed his counselor to check off scholarship paperwork that had been submitted during the current week, which Garlin brought back home every Friday. I even offered to provide self-addressed, stamped envelopes if necessary! (But fortunately for me, the school didn't need them.)

The Senior Year: Your Full Time Job!

The senior year is a whirlwind of activity designed to get your child to the next level in life. If you've done your job over the last 17 or 18 years, it can be a joyous time, the final push, the capstone of hard work for both you and your child. In this last year, don't get tired. Keep pushing all the way through.

THE SENIOR YEAR: A SUMMARY OF CRITICAL TASKS

❖ Be completely immersed in helping to prepare your child for their post-high school education. Whether it is college, trade school, or other training, it is your job to make sure that your child is prepared to step into their future immediately upon graduation. That means you are:

- ◆ For non-college bound students: Working with the school to identify apprenticeships, internships or community college training that can lead to skilled trades or service careers. Find out the requirements and make sure that your child can meet them.

- ◆ For the college-bound: Visiting colleges in person and on-line to see what the options are, and helping your child navigate the application process.

- ◆ For both: planning with your child how the post-high school training will be funded: probably a combination of loans, grants, scholarships, work and parental funding if you are able.

❖ Be organized! The process of discovering and funding post-high school education is involved. There are deadlines and timelines, and the bus will leave your child behind if you are not diligent.

❖ Continue to supervise your child's activities. In most cases, they are not legal adults, but they still reside in your household. Especially at prom time, make sure that you know where they are going, and continue to caution them about behavior.

Partnering With Your Child's Educator

See previous chapter.

SECTION THREE

College:
It's Different Now

CHAPTER 8

The College Game, Part I: Getting Ready

W hen I was in the 12th grade, my high school counselor, Mrs. Rebe Kingston, pulled me out of Economics class. "Sit down here and write me 500 words about what you want to be when you grow up, and why you want to go to college."

I wrote a little less than 500 words and gave them back to her. Next thing I knew, I had been awarded a special women's scholarship to Wayne State University (WSU): the Elliotorian Business Women's Club Annual Scholarship. Before I knew it, I had also been awarded the Wayne State University Board of Governor's Scholarship as well.

And so, off I went to college, that wonderful institution of higher learning, Wayne State University, a place where my hopes and dreams could come true if I prayerfully worked really hard to prepare myself for a bright and better future. As a result of Mrs. Kingston's help, I was the first girl in my family to graduate from college.

At that time—1974—the tuition for Wayne State University was probably about $500 per semester. That was a lot of money back then. But nothing like college costs now. Since 1974, college costs have increased an average of 2.5 to 3.5 percentage points *above* the annual inflation rate. College costs can range from about $7,000 per year in tuition and books, if your child stays home and commutes to school, to as much as $40-50,000 for tuition, room, and board for a private or Ivy League school.

So allow me to share with you "The Rules" when it comes to getting your son or daughter ready for college.

Rule #1: If you wait until 12th grade, you're already too late.

I have just walked you through preparing your child from pre-school through the 12th grade. By now, you should have deduced Rule #1 already. If you have followed these steps, if you have been truly engaged with your child and their education, social, emotional and religious support systems, then your child, now ready to leave the nest, or at least move on to their next phase in life, is on what I'd like to call the "Path to Purpose." That is absolutely where they will need to be if they are to be successful. After all, it's a different game now. Especially if they leave home for college, and I *highly* recommend that path if your child is mature enough to handle it, there will be no one there to ask every day, "Did you do your homework?" There will be no teachers calling or meeting with you on a regular basis to tell you how Johnny or Susie did on the test.

It's on the child now. How will they be able to motivate themselves to get through a challenging curriculum and navigate this new, more independent life?

It's easy. All they need is a purpose.

They may not have it right away. But hopefully you have groomed them and ingrained in them that they have a God-ordained reason for being on this earth, and that their number one priority is to first discover that purpose, and then to nurture it. Young adults who have a life purpose, or who are actively seeking what that might be, are going to be very, very motivated to do well so that their purpose might be realized.

It is interesting to watch this play out in the lives of those around you. A lot of adults are here on earth and have no idea what they're here on this earth to do, and that makes for a lot of unhappy people who go through life aimlessly, and often unsuccessfully. That is not what most parents want for their children. You want a child who has the joy, the "juice," the inner fortitude to keep on going, no matter what happens. Not just because they want to make money or have a big house—that's not purpose—but because they have a driving life mission. They may be good at ten things, but that ONE thing, that one true thing deep down on the inside, is what will keep them going, keep them meeting and overcoming challenges and obstacles, and make them thrilled to go to get up every morning to meet life anew each and every day for the rest of their lives.

Rule #2: NEVER rule out a college because of cost.

When I became involved with DAPCEP those many years ago, when Garlin was in the 5th grade, I made a decision to join their PAC. That was one of the best decisions I could have ever made.

"What committee do you want to join?" asked one of the parents at the first meeting that I attended. I looked at the choices, and decided on the Education Committee. After all, that's why I was there!

One of the first projects we executed was a College Fair. The Chair of the Education Committee worked for Ameritech, and so was able to secure donated conference space for our fair, along with snacks for the parents and college participants.

It was not hard to get colleges to participate in our fair; they knew about DAPCEP, and they wanted good students! At that first event, we were able to get several Michigan colleges, including the University of Michigan, Michigan State University, Wayne State University, Oakland University, and the University of Detroit (UD, now named UD-Mercy) to participate. We attracted more than 75 students and parents.

Remember, this was early in Garlin's educational life. A few people asked me, "Why that committee? Your son is YEARS away from college!"

138

My answer was simple: "He may not be close today, but he will be close tomorrow. I want to be prepared."

It was a fortuitous decision. After the event's activities were over, we were packing up to go home and I happened to strike up a conversation with a representative from the University of Michigan's Admissions Office. I was never shy when it came to my son's education.

This woman made an offhanded comment to me, and I credit that comment for motivating me to make sure that we would be able to handle college costs for Garlin, wherever he chose to attend. The comment was:

"Parents miss out on so much scholarship money because they're lazy."

"What do you mean, lazy?" I asked.

"Finding the money to go to college is an interactive process," she replied. "Scholarships do not come knocking on your door. You have to aggressively seek them, and go through quite a bit of trouble to secure them. You have to research, discover, call and ask for information, and then call and bug people if they don't send you what you need. And whatever they ask you to do, you must follow those instructions to the letter. A deadline is a deadline, and deadlines CANNOT be missed. Then you have to make sure that the colleges, or the scholarship organizations, received your information—that it didn't get lost in the mail or misplaced by someone. And then, after all that trouble, the response is often no. This can wear a person down and is simply too much trouble for most people, I find."

That conversation was a life-changing one for me.

"You don't have to worry about me," I told her. "I am a lot of things, but lazy is not one of them. When my son applies for scholarships, I WILL be in the game."

That was seven years before Garlin graduated from high school. I spent the next seven years learning, learning, and learning the college and scholarship game.

Her statement changed my life. That word, laziness, resonated with me and was the genesis of positioning my child, not just for financial success, but for emotional, educational, and career success. The next year, I chaired the Education Committee of PAC. I participated that year and continued every year for the next six years. Probably 600-800 children and their parents were exposed to those events during my tenure. And what I learned was invaluable.

One of the organizations I learned about was The National Society of Black Engineers (NSBE). As I mentioned earlier, it was just a few short years after learning about this supportive organization for African American engineers and engineer-aspirants that Garlin won the Golden Torch's Male High School Student of the Year Award from NSBE based on the one-inch thick portfolio that I had been building since his elementary school years.

But if I hadn't been friendly, if I hadn't been curious and interested and engaged, I never would have heard that statement.

I wish I knew that woman's name. I never saw her again. We just had that one critical conversation. I believe that she was sent from heaven to plant a seed in me, a seed that has watered many, many others who have been willing to listen. She redefined my work ethic when it came to parental involvement. The conversation didn't last long, but it altered the trajectory of my life and, consequently, my son's life. For that I thank God.

If you Google the term "unclaimed scholarships," you will get more than 600,000 hits. But the term "unclaimed" is really a misnomer. Available scholarships that no one receives are not unclaimed, because no one really has a claim on any individual scholarship. The better term is "un-worked for." No one who was eligible actually took the time to do the work to discover and pursue that given opportunity.

JUST KNOCK! Even after you get their package, ask for more.

Rule #3: GET and STAY organized.

Writing—and Organizing— for Admissions and for Dollars

By the time we got to Garlin's senior year, our family had a system and was able to apply to colleges as well as hundreds of scholarships. I had a very organized system and we cranked the applications out, working closely with his high school counseling staff.

The important thing is, we did not rely 100% on the high school counselors to navigate this process for us. Remember that they have their own caseloads! They cannot spend 10-20 hours a week helping your child. That is YOUR job.

As I began my research, I found that there were about six common college and scholarship essay topics. I had Garlin write six different personal statement essays during the summer before senior year of high school, and we pulled from those foundational essays to fit the various essay questions encountered on college admissions or scholarship applications. Once you complete two or three college or scholarship applications, you have pretty much all the information you need to complete an unlimited number of them. It's all about getting your own efficient system together.

I was the chief family clerk in charge. I kept track of deadlines and of the list of items needed for each application or scholarship package. I had a standard transmittal letter that I sent to the high school counselor every time we applied for a scholarship. I made it idiot-proof and work-proof for the counselor, who was extremely busy working with a large number of seniors. I created a turnkey package, such that all his counselor had to do was sign and return the required documents in the application process. This process put us light years ahead of the majority of other applicants. In fact, Garlin's counselor would say to me, "Mrs. Gilchrist, you don't have to do another thing, it's all under control." But I had a check off list for him that allowed me to do the proper follow up and make sure that all 'i's' were dotted and 't's' were crossed. I even had folders ready, with envelopes pre-addressed. "Do you need postage on this?" I would ask (He didn't). The school had to actually send copies of Garlin's official transcripts and high school principal, teacher or counselor letters of recommendation themselves, but I had everything else ready to go.

The result? *Garlin received more than $750,000 worth of scholarship money.* These monies came from countless colleges and universities, offering everything from full tuition, books, fees and room and board…to different cash scholarships ranging from $500 to $25,000 each. Garlin won several scholarships from the University of Michigan, which allowed him to attend college at no cost to us for college tuition, course books, classroom fees, room and board as well as all of his other living expenses for the entire five years he was at U-M obtaining two Engineering degrees. What a blessing!

We had always told our son that the Lord had destined him for greatness and that he could go has far as his heart and mind would take him. A big part of that destiny meant going to college. Now, I knew what my checkbook looked like. I had not been a good steward of the many blessings that the Lord had bestowed upon me. In other words, I had not been a very good steward of my money. I had not saved enough and I had too many credit cards. I must be honest and tell you that this brought me shame.

I wondered how I let myself get into this predicament. The answer, of course, was quite clear: I had spent too much and saved too little. Now I needed a miracle from the Lord to help me send my son to college without encumbering him with mountains and mountains of student loan debt. Neither did I want to encumber myself with the stress and strain of taking out a second mortgage on our home, borrowing from our 401(K) stock programs or co-signing for student loans. NO! All of those were horrendous choices as far as I was concerned. And while I understand that this may work for some, it was not going to work for me. There just had to be a better way. Fortunately, the Lord showed us that better way.

As I share this with you, I have to say that my shame is now gone, because I am so grateful to God for blessing our family. Unquestionably, God gets all of the glory for our miracle. We had nothing. But our son wanted to go to some of the nation's best schools (University of Michigan, Stanford University, MIT, Northwestern, UCLA, just to name a few), all of which cost, at least for us, an insurmountable fortune.

And guess what, folks? Tuition was not the only college expense. We also needed to cover room and board, books, fees, travel between home and campus and plain ol' living expense money! It gives me a headache even today just to think about it.

I had been told that if we worked really hard, and believe me I was highly motivated (having no money does that to a person), there were scholarship dollars to be found in what was essentially a needle-in-a-haystack game of finding the dollars for college. "Well," I said to myself, "game on," and with that, I went to work.

Life is about choices. One can sit back and feel sorry or sad about needing and not having, or one can muster up some intestinal fortitude and get busy doing something about it. I chose the latter for my son and our family.

Today, the world is more competitive than ever. To position your child to achieve, it is not enough to achieve at the local, state or even national level alone. They will have to compete at a global level to be truly successful. In order to achieve that success, they must do well in their studies. Being at a college you love certainly helps! The end game is for our children to do so well that they overwhelm the competition, and to that end, we want to position them such that they overwhelm the college admissions and scholarship selection board decision-makers with our children's achievements and motivation.

Parents, if you don't want to mortgage your house and your life, you're going to have to roll up your sleeves and go to work. Not in the 12th grade. Not in the 11th grade, but almost from birth. Success feeds on success at every level. It instills confidence and a 'can do' work attitude and the work that you do as parents builds a foundation for your child to have a good life.

145

In the end, Garlin had multiple options and chose to attend the University of Michigan for college. Along with that choice came the blessing of full scholarship dollars from multiple sources that paid for all of his tuition, all of his books, all course fees, room and board, and all of his transportation costs; including travels to and from home, etc. Every penny of educational expense was covered and we truly thank the Lord for all of that tremendous blessing.

That's what we all want for our children, isn't it?

CHAPTER 9

The College Game, Part II: It's Not Over

Now, we're going to talk about college. It's an entirely different animal from K-12. In college, your relationship with your child changes; you become someone different to your child. But don't get it twisted; the work is not over.

It was his sophomore year, 2001, and Garlin was, as many young men do, struggling to find his way. Some students get the "first-year itch" in college. Garlin "itched" in his second year.

Having a very bright son is indeed something wonderful and special. But it has its parental challenges as well. I clearly understood that our job as watchful and adoring parents did not end at the entrance of the University of Michigan (UM). I knew that we needed to find a solid balance between allowing our son the space to experience greater independence and self-reliance versus staying in touch, so that we would know when something substantial went off the proverbial 'rails'.

School was humming along quite nicely. Freshman year had been a tremendous success, both academically and socially. Garlin's scholarships required that he maintain at least a 3.0 GPA and he was on the Dean's list. Socially, he had lots of good friends and, for the most part, they were as serious about their school work as he was. So, all was well.

As a mother, I had become accustomed to not seeing Garlin and only talking on the telephone for sure on Sunday afternoons. Any other times were gravy. We established a routine where either Garlin Sr. or I checked up on major coursework assignments like big exams or big papers and we liked listening to him tell us how things were going.

By the middle of his second year, Garlin hit one of those proverbial brick walls in the form of a really tough math course. Given that Garlin was an Engineering major, he was taking Calculus courses that I had no prayer of understanding. But I knew that he did. So, as I was listening, I could hear the struggle in my son's voice, and I knew that I needed to pay even closer attention.

At first he wasn't talking much. This was new, and therefore, in my mind it could not be good. I knew that I needed to find out what was going on.

Garlin Sr. and I went to campus. "We're coming to take you to dinner," was how I played that song. I needed to see my son, so that I could look into his eyes and know that he was alright. It turned out that all he needed was a little extra TLC from his mother.

What do I mean by that? I'm glad you asked.

Garlin was struggling with a tough Calculus class and hadn't quite figured out how to handle it. Sometimes that happens to our children. As parents, we have to stay focused and sensitive enough to know when we need to do something about it. Garlin Sr. even stepped in, going up to campus for one-on-one time with his son. He never would tell me what those sessions were about. It was a man-to-man thing, and the woman in the room had to stay out. The Mom part of my conversation with Garlin focused on 'when the going gets tough, the tough get going.' I repeated my message that there was absolutely no shame in needing help.

No one is perfect, I told Garlin. We all need help of one kind or another in life. The problem is in *not getting* the help or assistance needed. People are not mind readers. They won't know what you need unless or until you tell them. I also reminded him that he was on academic scholarship, and that he did *not* have the luxury of slipping! Believe me when I tell you that my son understood exactly what I was saying.

What happened? Garlin discovered an office in the school called the Minority Engineering Program Office (MEPO, now known as the Multicultural Engineering Programs Office). As it turns out, MEPO had a Study Lab, complete with instructor office hours. Garlin rediscovered the fact that it was okay to reach out when something doesn't automatically click for you. I was so relieved and grateful when he started to benefit from all of this.

But I have to say, I also emphasized that a little too much partying might be going on and all that nonsense had to stop. All I can tell you for sure is that something must have changed, because the homework and test scores improved dramatically and we never missed a scholarship payment. That's enough to be thankful for all by itself.

The takeaway here is that college is not just "Grade 13." This is not a time to leave your child to their own devices. Sure, they're in college, and technically (if they're 18) adults, but you still have *work* to do.

But your work role now shifts. You are a counselor from afar. You don't have nearly the control that you had when they were home (even if they're still living at home). But if you've raised your child correctly, they should be ready, and will be open to your loving parental influence and guidance well into their adult years. You give input, but ultimately they have to make up their own minds now. Your role is to simply help them make informed choices.

When Garlin left home for the University of Michigan, I wondered, "How am I going to let go?" I had feelings of loss. This was my baby and my buddy. At age 17, he was leaving home and becoming a full-grown man. For the first time in my life, I would have absolutely no idea what he was doing, where he was, or who he was doing it with. Up until this point, I never had a conscious moment when I didn't know where he was supposed to be. All of that was changing. I knew he would be fine. He would make lots of friends. He was going to the university that he wanted to go to. He would get great support. He would help others.

The question was, would I "be fine?" After all, there would be a loss. If you're a parent, you know what I'm talking about.

I had to pray and ask God to minimize that sense of loss. He told me that I wasn't losing my child. He was just transitioning to manhood.

I would have to learn to transition my attitude. I was dealing with an independent young man. I could not control things around him anymore, because I would not be seeing him every day.

How did I do? Better than I expected. I think I know why.

First, I was settled in my spirit. I was at peace. I knew in the deepest recesses of my being that I had done everything that I possibly could have done for my child.

Second, I was a whole person when I started this journey with Garlin. For the first seventeen years, from conception until he left for school, I had my own life. My son was absolutely a priority for me. While I gave all to him that was 'givable,' I still kept compartments for my other roles in life. I also had to be there for my husband, my family, my profession…and myself. I was evolving professionally, having developed my own educational consulting firm. I was called into the ministry and had that gift and call to develop. All of this was going on at the same time I was pouring into Garlin. So I was complete, full and satisfied. I felt like God had given me an awesome assignment, the most important responsibility I'd ever had in my life, which was to raise Garlin in the nurture and admonition of the Lord. So now, I could walk away in peace...almost.

I have to admit that I did not respond well to Garlin's second-year lapse. I wrote a scathing, epithet-filled letter. Mothers, you understand. Fathers, you understand. Sometimes your child just makes you go there. And I did go there.

I no longer have a copy of that fated letter. Maybe it wasn't meant for me to find. It was a "Moses"-style letter, full of warnings, but also full of blessings and confidence as I emphasized to Garlin that he was God's child and destined to be successful and make an impact.

That's what I want to emphasize to you. We must give our children a balanced view of life. Life is full of dangers and possible wrong turns, and they must be made aware of that unfortunate fact. Yet, they also stand to benefit from a future of untold blessings, but only if they follow the right track.

> *"Today I'm giving you the choice of a blessing or a curse." (God speaking to the Israelites upon their entering the Promised Land)*
>
> *~Deuteronomy 11:26 (God's Word)*

152

Close One Chapter, Open Another One: How to Successfully Interact with Your Adult Child

Garlin and I went very quickly from mother-and-son to partners. I came to grips with the fact that, in this partnership, I was not the one that was going to be in control. Now that he was no longer under my roof, I couldn't order him around. So what did that partnership mean?

For me, it meant remaining engaged and concerned—but now from a distance. It meant always communicating that Garlin was loved and respected, and that we remained concerned. We sent him a clear message. "Our doors, our telephone, our hearts are available to you 24/7. You can call anytime. You can come home anytime. And this is our gift to you—the benefit of our journey in life, so that we can help you navigate your path. We want to provide trusted input. We're qualified to do that because of the time we've spent on this earth, the roads we've traveled and the mistakes we've made. But at the end of the day, son, we leave all final decisions to you. Grown men choose their own path."

My husband and I made it clear to Garlin that it was incumbent upon him to figure out what advice he would take, and what he would not. On HIM, not on US.

The "Arms Length" Parent

I was not confused. I knew that going to this prestigious university was no joke. I couldn't let him just flounder. So we parented, but at arm's length. We were going to make

153

sure that Garlin had the benefit of that knowledge, whether he wanted it or not. We didn't raise a fool. Garlin, for the most part, received our advice and considered it seriously. Most of the time, he made well thought-out decisions that we could live with. They were not always the decisions that we wanted him to make, but they were well-thought-out nonetheless.

We gave him a few important pieces of parting advice. "Don't ever, ever leave a drink unattended. Not a Pepsi, Sprite, 7 Up, or anything else. When you purchase a drink, you drink all of it. Don't put it down and pick it back up later. You have enough money; you can afford to buy another one," I would tell him. I would never want money to stand in the way of his safety.

Life-and-death matters are just that, and oh so important. Let them know to back out of danger; in dangerous parties, unsafe gatherings, etc. Flee from danger, no matter what. Do not get in trouble trying to be cool. Always beware of the folks who try to tear you down.

Another important step we took with Garlin was to review his class schedule at registration time. This was critical initially. I know too many students who never recover from a bad first year. They took too many classes or too many 'hard' classes freshman year, got terrible grades, and their GPAs simply never recovered. We would conference call with Garlin to review his syllabi and talked to him about his course load.

What do I mean? Here's an example. Let's say he had a Chemistry class, and there were three tests and some lab work associated with that class. We would ask him when the first test was. In the beginning, we didn't wait for him to call us, we'd call him. We had the dates in hand, and would ask him, "Don't you have a test coming up? Are you ready? Do you need extra help?" Right from the beginning, we would ask, "How are classes going?" It took more than, "Okay." We wanted DETAILS, and we asked for them.

There are all kinds of barriers: tough subjects, language challenges and sometimes even bad teachers. We encouraged him to go to his professors' office hours. We encouraged him to meet frequently with his teachers. The squeaky wheel gets the grease and the student who makes the most noise with his or her professor (assuming that the "noise" consists of intelligent and thoughtful questions that clearly indicate that they have done some work before approaching the professor) gets the benefit of the doubt. We encouraged him to get to know his professors and teaching assistants in every class.

We also encouraged him to participate in study groups. A lot of students are reluctant to do that because a) they don't think it's necessary; or b) they are intimidated by their fellow students. They may feel as if those students are smarter than they are, and will look down on them if they don't measure up. Others are rugged individualists, believing that if they got into the school, then they should be able to figure it out without depending on other people. A third group feels that they already know everything and don't need to study with anyone else.

All of these positions are just plain wrong. You must let your child know that it is not just okay, but absolutely necessary, to seek and accept help wherever it can be found. And those "smart" students? Many of them got that way precisely because they had been acculturated to assertively and deliberately look to peers, parents, and instructors alike for the academic help and any support that they needed.

Know Your Child—Take Action if Necessary

As a parent, you have to be sensitive to when there might be a problem, even if your child does not tell you. You might need to help them manage. Bring things up:

"I haven't heard anything about that Physics class."

"I got a 'C'".

"Maybe you need a tutor. Where can you get one?"

You have to communicate to your child again and again that there's nothing wrong with them getting help, and that accepting help is perfectly okay. Tell them, "Today, you may need help. Tomorrow, you'll be able to help someone else."

In his junior year, Garlin bumped into a really tough class, and so this time I found a tutor: Dr. Anthony Will. He worked in my company at the GM Tech Center, and he went to our church.

"Garlin is struggling," I told him. "I don't know what's going on, but he's not talking. I want you to call him."

I also talked to another young man, Greg Posey, a University of Michigan Engineering graduate who had worked with me in DAPCEP. I called him up and let him know what was going on. "You need to help him," I said.

"Garlin hasn't called me," Greg responded.

"I know! That's the problem. You need to find out what's going on, because I know it's something."

Sometimes you have to force the issue. I was one who had no shame when it came to my child! He was on scholarship, and he *had* to keep that money. Why would I not intervene?

Greg responded to Garlin's "squeaky wheel" mom. Garlin ended up studying with Greg at his apartment, which was driving distance from his Ann Arbor dorm. Greg was able to ferret out the source of his struggles, and Garlin was able to get through. He ended up with an A in the class.

It was worth it. Garlin got his 'swag' back.

All I'm saying parents, is that you need to tune in. Get to know what's happening on your child's campus. Get to know the educational resources and people on campus. Get to know the dean, the counselor, and make yourself known, so that you can intervene effectively if necessary. The college faculty and staff should know that there is *somebody* who cares about this child. I'm not talking about being intrusive or always in the way. Exercise your influence only when necessary, but when necessary parents, please exercise!

Talk to your child often. This is a difficult subject, but relevant nonetheless. On a practical note, make sure that they're making sense. Know the signs of substance abuse.

More importantly, know your child's signs. As a parent, you know when something is off. If you pick up danger signals, you need to investigate them. You should have been talking to them all along, remember? Prayerfully, this will never happen to your child, but stay on your Ps and Qs…and your knees!

So, your child is moving toward independence in college, but you have to still be aware of what's going on with them, and listen to your parent's intuition when you sense a problem or challenge. Then, it is okay to get them the support they need, to get them in front of someone that can help if that someone is not you.

There is a Difference

In grades K-12, as a parent, you are there all the time for your child. Once they're in college, your role changes. I like to call the college parent's role "temporary angel."

You will have to do a delicate dance in college with your child. You'll necessarily be a bit lighter on your feet, not as heavy-handed, and flexible enough to know when to intervene and when to step back, when to just give encouragement and when to do an old-fashioned TAKEOVER (those times should be never or few and far between, if you've done your parenting job well).

There is one key difference in your parenting of a college son or daughter: your intervention, if it has to happen at all, only has to be for a *season*. When your child is back on track, that is your clue to back *out*. Just take a look at this passage that reveals God's heart for His children:

> *"Because he loves me," says the LORD, "I will rescue him;*
> *I will protect him, for he acknowledges my name.*
> *He will call on me, and I will answer him;*
> *I will be with him in trouble,*
> *I will deliver him...*

> *~Psalm 91:14-15a* (NIV)

God rescues us in trouble. We should do no less for our children. Just know that sometimes you will have to rescue them before they actually humble themselves enough to call on you.

And that's okay too.

SECTION FOUR

The Portfolio–
The Key to Your
Child's Success
From the Inside Out!

Remember the NSBE GTA Award that I talked about at the beginning of Part II? That was just the beginning. Garlin went on to win more than three-quarters of a million dollars in scholarships to colleges and universities nationwide. He was able to select and attend the college of his choice, the University of Michigan. His father and I did not have to spend a dime on tuition, fees or ANY living expenses. Five years later, he graduated from the University of Michigan College of Engineering with two engineering degrees...and no debt! We are so thankful. And looking back, it was more than worth the effort.

Parents, I want you to position your child for success so that you—and your child—can have similar moments of pride and share wonderful testimonies. I hope that you have seen throughout the book that this takes hard work on your part, and a commitment to never give up.

I started Garlin's portfolio when he was in grade school. I accumulated and organized the records so that when I needed them I could draw on them and all the information was at my fingertips.

My story can be your story. It is a story of hard but joyous and purposeful sacrifice, a story with a happy ending.

Are you convinced? Let's get to work.

CHAPTER 10

What Goes in Your Portfolio?

The Portfolio is a **living** document. It will change and grow with your child.

The Portfolio is an **adaptable** document. You will be able to mix and match the sections to fit virtually any purpose.

The Portfolio is a **unique** document. There will be commonalities, but different children will have different interests and experiences to highlight and document.

The Portfolio is a **positioning** document. It puts your child in a position to receive the opportunities that can be garnered when they can concretely show a full, multifaceted experience in addition to academic achievement and/or improvement from grades K-12 and beyond.

POSITIONING YOUR CHILD FOR SUCCESS

The Portfolio is a **powerful** document. It can help develop self-esteem. It can mark memory. It can be passed down through the generations.

At the pre-school and early elementary levels, your child's portfolio is very simple. The items you put in relate to your child's everyday life, and therefore are very easy to explain to your child and others. It is then equally as easy and enjoyable for your child to actively participate, and gain firsthand experience, in the art of organizing things related to themselves, their family, and the world around them.

I'll show you a full sample outline later in this chapter.

Make sure, too, that you share the portfolio often with family and friends. It makes your child proud when you show others their special "book." Even when they get older and don't want to admit it, the portfolio becomes a permanent source of pride in personal accomplishments. It is also a good idea to place the portfolio in an easily accessible location to your child. This way they can also share their wonderful portfolio and the things contained inside with family and friends. Grandparents, aunts, uncles, and other extended family members and close friends are often the first persons to hear this good news about your child's portfolio.

"Grandma, Grandma, I can't wait until you come over so that I can show you my latest portfolio update!"

In later grades, and especially in high school, the portfolio gets more complicated. You will get more sophisticated about how you organize your child's documentation. You will find that tabbed dividers help, as well as folders with three-ringed holes to put into binders.

Next, I am going to give you some essential outlines. The first will be your "Child ID Kit." This is what you put together even before the portfolio, and it is a way to safeguard your child's identity and make sure you have essential information at your fingertips when you need it.

The second is a laundry list of items you MAY put into the Portfolio of your pre-K-6 child. This is a pretty exhaustive list, and you should not feel obligated to try and find items for every single category. This is a guideline and a trigger to help you think through developing your child's unique portfolio profile.

The third is the more comprehensive portfolio for your child in grades 7-12. This is where you become much more detailed; your child will start to participate in more structured activities and programs, and you'll have a lot more to pull from when you are ready to do the portfolio "subsets": the Specialized and the Targeted Portfolios.

Finally, we'll bring this discussion up to the Digital Age and address the electronic tools that you can use…and provide some caveats to that as well.

Child ID Kit

Birth certificate

Fingerprints and footprints

Medical records (i.e., immunization, health, dental)

Social Security Card

Financial Records

This type of information should be kept in a separate folder or envelope marked "Confidential." Identity theft is rampant and growing every day, so you have to be especially cautious! One can never be too careful in this regard. Be safe and err on the side of caution.

However, you will need to provide a copy (never give the original to anyone) of your child's birth certificate in certain instances. When the child starts school, they will need a birth certificate. Should you choose to allow your child to participate in organized sports, they will need a copy of their birth certificate along with the proper immunization records. This information verifies who the child is, the child's age, and confirms that the appropriate health department immunizations have been secured and it is safe for your child to participate in sports activities. To get around the confidentiality issue, make a copy of the original birth certificate, then blackout any confidential information that has been printed on the document, such as the parents' Social Security numbers or other non-essential information that does not relate to the child. No one needs that information, unless they can explain specifically why and how they plan to use it.

Make at least 5 or 10 copies of that 'modified' birth certificate. Place the original, and then the copies, in a sheet protector. This is the document that you give to anyone legitimately asking for a copy of your child's birth certificate. You now have a readily available document when asked to provide it. Because you are now organized and your child's personal documents are in a safe and secure location, you know where to find them when needed and you will only give officials what they truly need—your child's information, not information pertaining to you or your spouse.

Supply List

- ♦ Three-Ringed Binder
- ♦ Sheet Protectors (at least 10)
- ♦ Tabbed Dividers with Table of Contents
- ♦ Portfolio (for art samples and larger projects)

General Portfolio—Pre-K-6

At this level, you'll probably want to incorporate tabbed dividers because you will have multiple documents in numerous categories.

Attendance certificates

Achievement certificates

Class pictures

Class awards

Individual awards

First day or other school mementos

Journal writings

First resume

Creative projects—drawing, painting, pottery, etc.

Photographs/Videos (child, family, friends)

Books read

Samples of class projects

Program acceptance letters or certificates of completion

Library card

Theatre/Movie/Museum ticket stubs

Places I've been / things I've done

Anything else valued by you or your child that you wish to save!

General Portfolio—Grades 7-12

At this level, you will probably want to incorporate a few more tabbed dividers.

Academic records

Awards and/or certificates

Resume

First paycheck stub

Programs or certificates of completion

What Goes In Your Portfolio?

Places I've been / things I've done

Books read

Class projects or inventions—samples or summaries

Writings

Drawings, paintings, creations, etc.

Activities, hobbies, mementos

Photographs / Videos

Media documentation

What Do You Mean?

Below, I explain some of the items I have mentioned above, so that you are clear on exactly what kinds of items belong in each category:

Academic Records—These are your official school records: report cards, standardized test scores, and progress reports.

Awards and Certificates—Individual or group recognition or achievement. Examples include school awards, *community* service recognition, recognition or participation certificates from religious affiliations, etc. If one of your children comes home with a star on their forehead, take a picture of that child and label it! It's a great way to celebrate accomplishment. Remember: if your child's school doesn't distribute awards or certificates in

171

earlier grades, at the appropriate time and for the appropriate reason, discuss this with your child's teacher to ask if some type of recognition or achievement award/certificate could be prepared. It would be helpful if you brought samples or suggestions that would benefit, not only your child, but the entire class.

Programs—Keep track of the school and/or community programs in which your child participates. Be sure to keep an extra copy or two of those programs that have your child's name printed on them. These programs will come in handy later on when you need to use those experiences as morale boosters. The printed program also serves as your documentation that your child participated in a particular program.

Outings and Events ("Things We've Done and Places We've Been")—To document the places you've been and things your child has done, or that you have done as a family. I must admit that this point was inspired by Dr. Ben Carson's story, where he records that his mother, who was not highly educated, made he and his brother read a book every week and write a book report—before they could enjoy television privileges. She found a way to find occasions and opportunities for learning.

This category is about recognizing and honoring the vastness of your child's experiences. It's about helping them to appreciate the joy of the everyday. If you see a movie that's significant, save the ticket stub! If you go to the park, take a picture of your child in the park. It may be just the inspiration your child needs when they have to think of an essay topic or science fair project, for example.

And by the way, it's a great way to give your little one something to do when they're bored. "Remember when you went to see The Lion King?" you'll tell them, pulling out the portfolio and its accompanying ticket stub. "Why don't you draw a picture about it, or write a story about it? Who were the main characters? Which ones did you like best? Why? Which ones didn't you like? Why? What was the most important thing about the movie to you, and why? Would you change anything about the movie, or the characters?" Upon completion, ask your child to read or enact the story they just wrote. You could even ask them to rewrite the ending, or add a character and tell the story a different way. What does this promote? Reading and writing skills. Comprehension skills. Performance skills. Public speaking skills. And it eliminates the boredom, plus frees up time for you.

At the younger ages, they'll be thrilled to do this, and hear you "ooh" and "aah" over what they have done. Challenge your child, even at young ages, to record as much detail as possible. "What color were the seats? What did the theater look like? What row did you sit in at the show? Did you enjoy the music? Do you remember any of the words to the songs?

Are you challenged with reviewing your child's writing for grammar, correct spelling and accuracy? No shame in that. Ask their teacher, or a friend or family member that you trust, to review the writing for you.

This is a great opportunity for your child to meet their destiny by creating fun, unique learning activities in the home. You're helping them to shape their ability to read and write, to listen, to speak, to count, and they don't even know it! All they know is that they're engaging in activities; they're not bored. Learning does not just take place at the schoolhouse; life is a wonderful and dynamic classroom, and it starts with you, the parent. After all, home is the FIRST vital classroom of your child's life, and you can make it a natural classroom, where learning is so infused into your child's home life that the classroom is just a natural extension of what you're already doing with them at home. This is another important and fun way to develop your child's reading, writing, critical thinking and speaking skills. This is non-threatening activity; you're helping your child communicate as a matter of course, and over time it becomes second nature for them.

Photographs/Videos—While events and activities document environment, pictures go a bit deeper. They also document sentiments and feelings, which are so important and valuable to our children, and will be to their children's children as well. Close your eyes and picture your child, 70 years old, talking with their grandchildren: "This is the time that your great-granddaddy took me to a science program, and that's when I decided I wanted to go into research." Or, "This is where your great-grandparents took me to Sea World Amusement Park, and I have loved the water ever since."

But back to the present. Young children are ego-centric; that means they think about themselves first. When they are young, say from about 3 to 6 years of age, they see those pictures and look for themselves. That satisfies them where they are. I call it the "see me" stage. This is perfectly fine at the younger ages; seeing themselves in photos is another way of conveying to them their worth to you as their parent.

Next, they start to think about family. "This is me with my Mommy or me with my Daddy, and we're at the beach." Great for show-and-tell days.

After that, grounded in the knowledge that they are loved and valued, they are able to start thinking about the wider community. "This is my team; we won first prize!"

Pictures are vital tools in your child's maturation process. The good feelings they have as they go back over and over again to look at the pictorial evidences of their growth and development over time will literally help drive their educational accomplishment and personal maturation.

We are in an unprecedented digital and video age, and it is more significant than ever to take pictures, and videos if possible, of everything in which your child is involved, from home life to school and extracurricular life. How I wish I had pictures of my parents as children, or even more, pictures of me and my siblings when we were young! Not to put too fine a point on it, but do not forget to list the given names of everyone in the picture (put nicknames in quotation marks), your child's age and grade level, the location where the picture was taken and the event or activity. You think you'll remember, but you won't. As a tip, do not write on the back of the photo itself. Instead, type or write the picture information and description on a label (you can get thousands of labels at the office supply store very economically).

Media Documentation—This is yet another way to document your child's success. Any time your child wins an award, an athletic competition, or is involved in significant extracurricular activities, trumpet it! You can write your own article on his or her success and send it to your local newspaper's community section. Look up the editor's email address on the newspaper's website and send it right in! Editors look for "good news" articles such as these, and they make impressive additions to your child's portfolio for any purpose, from acceptance into K-12 academic enrichment programs to college and scholarship applications. Your success at promoting your child will depend on a combination of your own assertiveness and ingenuity and the prevalence of multiple media outlets and feature opportunities. There may be large urban newspapers in your community, small local papers or tabloids, a public television outlet, a public radio outlet, and/or cable television "public access" channels.

This is truly a case of the squeakiest wheel getting the grease. In Detroit, a local television station promotes a high school Athlete of the Week. If you were in the Detroit area, and had a child who was excelling academically and athletically, you might contact the producer of that show. They are not hard to find; all you have to do is call the station and ask. You can trot your portfolio down to that station and see about opportunities to feature your child; or better yet, you might get in touch with your child's coach and ask them to assist you.

There are a number of small suburban newspapers that actually look for local good news articles. I connected with one of those papers and decided to make their work easier. Whenever Garlin had an accomplishment in school or in sports, I would write it up. I researched the information and submitted the article along with pictures. The paper's editors would edit the information to fit their needs; or sometimes they would include the article in its entirety. But no matter what, I would always be careful to give them MORE than they needed—the formal name of the program, the program purpose, the dates the program ran, the director of the program and the institution or organization in which the program was housed.

If Garlin got accepted into a competitive academic program for example, I would find out how many students applied and how many got accepted, and work that data into the article, along with any accomplishments Garlin may have achieved in the program. If you don't feel comfortable preparing such a story for your child, again, get someone to help you. It can be a family member, a friend, or even your child's teacher. It is critically important to give the editors what they need; they will appreciate you. Eventually the newspaper editors would call me to ask, "What is Garlin doing these days?" I always gave a detailed response!

You are, in essence, becoming your child's public relations expert. As such, integrity and accuracy are essential. Your facts must be accurate so that the newspaper's fact-checkers will, each and every time, be able to verify the information you provide.

For exceptional success stories, you might even want to look at national publications. Specialty ethnic publications such as *Ebony* and *Jet*, or inserts like *Parade* magazine, will sometimes feature an outstanding student who has a nationally-recognized award or multiple outstanding achievements. Again, all it will cost you is some effort and the time that it takes to make a phone call. The payoff could be substantial.

When I was doing all of this for Garlin in the 1990s, it was a different world. Email and the Internet were fairly new phenomena, and there was no such thing as Social Media. Since the turn of the century, options for promoting anything and anyone have exploded. You must stay abreast of those opportunities. You should also:

Make sure your child's Facebook page includes their accomplishments. You must convey to them that college recruiters and employers alike use social media sites like Facebook in their selection processes now. If they post a picture of themselves obviously drunk, or scantily dressed, it's not only their friends that know it; potential employers and college administrators will too! If they tell you that they keep their page "private," impress upon them that NOTHING is private today. The cardinal rule: never put anything in social media cyberspace that you would be embarrassed if the entire world saw or knew, because, one day, they just might!"

Videotape your child's sports accomplishments, music or speaking performances and award ceremonies and upload them to YouTube if you are so inclined. It is very simple for you to put the YouTube link to your child's performance on a resume.

Create a PowerPoint or other digital version of your child's portfolio. That moves the portfolio from a one-dimensional hard-copy binder to a dynamic, multimedia vehicle by which you can 'wow' recruiters. You can place audio and video recordings of your child, or create unique animations or music that add interest. The possibilities are endless! The most proactive parents (and their children, who are typically much more electronically savvy) are already creating these kinds of creative products to position them at the head of the line for acceptance into pre-college programs, colleges, scholarships and awards.

Once you have this "kitchen sink" portfolio, you are in an excellent position to build the more tailored versions.

The Specialized Portfolio

Is your child especially talented in the arts? Are they enthusiastic about writing? Math games? Animals? Those activities will certainly be included in the General Portfolio; but if you find your child has a keen interest in a topic, you will be looking for ways to increase their exposure. As you do that, you will create more and more items to include in a smaller, more focused portfolio that documents their particular interest.

Let's say the interest is animals. You might include pictures of your child horseback riding, an essay they wrote on dogs, video of them engaged in training their dog, veterinary records, 4H awards…you get the picture.

The Targeted Portfolio

The Targeted Portfolio is designed to position your child for a certain program, scholarship opportunity, internship experience and the like. Are you helping your child obtain a special volunteer assignment like March of Dimes? You would need to demonstrate their experience in/capacity for compassionate service. Are they applying to become a tutor for younger grades? You want to show academic prowess, and perhaps past experience (maybe they helped their younger sibling with a homework assignment and impact their grade). Are they trying to win a place on a prestigious Amateur Athletic Union (AAU) team? Are they trying to obtain a scholarship? Are they auditioning for an acting part in a film or a play? For any of these examples, you can pull from the larger portfolio to help create one that directly answers why your child is especially qualified to be chosen for one particular opportunity.

~

This is just a partial list of what to include in your child's portfolio, and how to make sure your child is in the best position to be recognized and rewarded for their accomplishments. You will surely, as you develop this, think of other items to include that are unique to your child and your family.

Let me emphasize that you must do the legwork. It is no one's job to promote your child except you. To position your child for success, you must be relentless in making it happen. Others will help you, but no one is obligated to do

180

the job for you, nor do they have the time or the resources. It is you who must be the driving force.

The greatest joy will be when you share this with your grandchildren. The portfolio is a generational blessing, as your children see first-hand and in detail their rich heritage and model the wisdom found between the covers of this very special binder.

If you do this right, your child will drive the portfolio process. How to do it right? Bring them in! Don't make it a do-it-yourself project. Explain all of the sections. Ask them where they think a particular picture or document should be filed. Keep it visible, so that when auntie, uncle, grandma, or grandpa comes over, your child will grab their hand and pull them toward this important documentation.

You will know you've got it right when they say to you after some activity, accomplishment, or event, "Mom/Dad, this should go into my portfolio!" You are telling your child that they are worth the time it takes to carefully craft this documentation of their life. They know that they have value in this unit called "family," and that in this fast-paced, no-time-to-do-anything world, you have seen fit to take time out of your busy schedule to chronicle every aspect of your child's life, for a record that will last throughout generations.

Your Portfolio Kit

Are you convinced yet? Yes? Here are some additional tips:

POSITIONING YOUR CHILD FOR SUCCESS

First things first

You absolutely MUST designate a certain place where all of your child's portfolio items will be safely stored until they can be placed. This temporary place can be a large drawer, a plastic bin, an elaborate filing system, or even a section of a closet, but it must be one spot, a spot where the items will be safe as long as you live there. A damp basement is NOT eligible! Make sure that you use a spot that you will be able to remember, so you won't go around saying, "Where did I put that certificate?"

If you're just starting out, get a big box in which to put everything.

With that done, it's time to format. A good beginning system to use is a three-ringed, tabbed binder along with dividers and sheet protectors. Tabbed dividers allow you to list your categories in a table of contents that you create and place in the front of your binder. I suggest the dividers with five tabs, so that you have enough room to write the category on each tab. Buy as many sheet protectors as you can afford, so you don't have to keep going back. A box of 50-100 is a good number to begin with.

Now, start with the categories mentioned above (according to your child's grade level) and begin filling out your table of contents based on the categories we discussed that apply to your child/family. Get a large quantity of three-hole punch sheet protectors. The sheet protectors allow for ease in handling the documents placed in the portfolio, and serve to protect your documents against deterioration or damage to your originals.

It's Okay to Be a Pack Rat

In this instance, it's actually good to hoard important things. That attendance award from fourth grade. That church certificate for Vacation Bible School. The piece of art that won first prize in the school contest. You never know what you may use that will be the very item that tips the scales in your child's favor for a competitive summer program, a music scholarship, or that singular college that is looking for a certain category of student to round out their enrollment.

The Portfolio charts your child's growth and achievements. This not only gives you a sentimental look at how far your child has come, but also will enable you to keep track of important documents for future use. It also gives your child a tangible look into how much they have accomplished and shows how they have built a strong foundation in many areas. They help the child do a "self-inventory" and mentally project into the future.

Got it? Start small, start now, and don't be intimidated. It's never too late!

CHAPTER 11

The Winning Resume: Your Child's Power Tool for Careering

A resume? For a child? How does that work?

It certainly is not a laundry list of jobs and career accomplishments. At its most basic form, a resume is simply a chronicle and summary of your child's valuable experiences (think: overseas travel or participation in a spelling bee), special skills (think: knowledge of Microsoft Word or website design), community service work (think: tutoring younger students or working in a soup kitchen), and examples of demonstrated leadership (think: student council representative or sports team captain). Done right, it can be extremely effective in getting your child to the top of the list for various competitive opportunities, from educational programs to scholarships to college.

If you began this process when your child was in elementary or middle-school, you should by now have a fairly thick portfolio with rich information on your child's experiences and accomplishments. That portfolio is both chronological, and divided into various academic and activity categories. You will now use it to create your child's resume, organized by the categories into which your portfolio is divided. With the hard work you've already done over the years, it should be fairly easy to prepare.

The following is Garlin's senior year resume, the one that helped secure for him more than $750,000 in scholarships and entry into the University of Michigan:

RESUME OF GARLIN GILCHRIST
Address
City, State, Zip Code
Telephone   E-Mail Address

EDUCATION

Farmington High School
32000 Shiawassee
Farmington, MI 48336-3251   **3.96 Cumulative GPA**

EXPERIENCE/TECHNICAL SKILLS

Laboratory Research Assistant   June-August 1999

Wayne State University, Minority High School Science
Education Program   Location: Detroit, MI

> Participating in this summer program allowed me to hold my
> first paid position. I worked as a research assistant for an
> established professor in psychiatry, Dr. Randall L.
> Commissaris. Along with Dr. Commissaris and an
> undergraduate lab assistant, I researched anxiety-like
> behavior in specially bred rats. This allowed me to work with
> a man at the head of his field, gain invaluable knowledge
> about scientific research, and to participate in the authoring of
> a published study. I received the award for Outstanding
> Research Assistant during the Summer of 1999.

Jr. Computer Consultant   1997-1998

Three Wonders of Computers
   Location: Southfield, MI

Utilizing the opportunity to learn from the owners and taking initiative on my own, I developed a high level capability for both building and troubleshooting personal computers, including Year Two Thousand (Y2K) compliance. Being well–versed in most Windows and Mac based applications, I am comfortable utilizing the BASIC, Visual Basic, and C++ programming languages, and using/teaching word processing applications, writing HTML code, desktop publishing, creating graphs and spreadsheets, editing photos, photo editing/manipulation, computer presentations, networking, and expertly navigating the Internet.

AWARDS

Detroit Association Phi Beta Kappa Certificate of Recognition, April 2000

National Society of Black Engineers (NSBE), Golden Torch Award, Pre-College Student of the Year 2000

National Achievement Scholarship Program, National Merit Commendation Award, Fall 1999

Michigan High School Athletic Association Scholar Athlete – Boys Basketball Grades 11 and 12

Who's Who in Sports: High School Division, 1997, 1998, and 1999

National Ventures Scholar, May 1999

Detroit Urban League, Member 1999, 2000

National Consortium for Academics and Sports, National Collegiate Athletic Association

"National Student-Athlete Award", 1999 and 2000

Presidential Classroom Scholar, February 1999

Farmington High School, Academic Letter Award, Grades 9, 10, 11 & 12

Who's Who Among American High School Students, 1997, 1998, 1999 & 2000

Mann Elementary School, After School Tutorial Program, "Outstanding Youth Tutor", 1997, 1998, 1999

Mann Elementary School, After School Mentoring Program, "Outstanding Youth Mentor", 1997, 1998, 1999

Mann Elementary School City of Detroit Youth Basketball, "Outstanding Youth Basketball Assistant Coach", 1997, 1998, 1999

Meals on Wheels, Detroit Area Center for the Aging, "Outstanding Volunteer Service", 1997, 1998, 1999, 2000

Lawrence Technological University, Lines and Curves, Mathematics Award, 1998

University of Michigan Summer Engineering Academy, Summer Apprenticeship Program, 1998

"Best Overall Academic Achievement in Mathematics and Technical Communications, 1998

Optimist International "Optimist Oratorical Contest" Silver Medalist, 1997

University of Michigan Summer Engineering Academy, Minority Introduction to Technology & Engineering,

"Outstanding Achievement in Communication Skills," 1997

Michigan Technological University Minorities in Engineering Workshop, Outstanding Achievement, 1997

University of Michigan Summer Engineering Academy, Summer Engineering Program II,

"Best Overall Academic Achievement in Mathematics and Science" 1996

ACTIVITIES/COMMUNITY SERVICE

NSBE 1999 Region IV Summer ConferenceNSBE PCI Leadership Conference, Yorkville, IL

Detroit Urban League, Inc.

College Club, Programs and Community Services (Grades 11 and 12, 1999)

Farmington Express Basketball TeamMI AAU, State Championship "All Star" 17 & Under (Grades 11, June, 1999)

Farmington High School Athletics:Varsity and JV Basketball Teams, Track & Field Team (Grades 9-11)

Optimist International Detroit Bicycle Safety Coach

(Summers, 1996 Through 1999)

Jam City Basketball Club of DetroitAmateur Athletics Union Basketball Team

Tabernacle Missionary Baptist ChurchSunday School

Chaplain, Leader of Church Youth Activities

Tabernacle Bus Ministry Assistant

> Transportation of wheelchair bound & elderly residents to & from church

Never Alone Christian Companion Program

> Volunteer Prayer, Bible Study & assistance with sick & shut-in persons

Campaign Volunteer, Southfield City Councilwoman: Sylvia Jordan

Meals On Wheels, Detroit Area Center For The Aging (1996 - Present)

Tutor, Mentor, Basketball Coach

Mann Elementary School, After School Tutorial Program

> Tutoring, Computer Software Training, Spanish, Language Arts, Math & Science

Detroit Area Pre-College Engineering Program

DAPCEP Saturday Program & Summer Engineering Academy

Radio Talk Show Youth Guest Host, Detroit WMKM "Making A Difference" Radio Talk Show Program (1998-1999)

DaimlerChrysler Corporation

> High School Mentorship Program (Grade 11)

Ford Motor Company High School Science &
Technology Program (Grade 10)

NAACP Life Time Member for Juniors

Veterans Freeman Home Community Service: Homeless
Shelter, Food & Clothing Distribution

SC Jones Community Center

Community Outreach: Tutoring & Assistance with
Computer Lab

References Available Upon Request

You can put this resume in the front of your child's
portfolio, and change it every time you add a substantial
item to the folder. Keep it on your computer so that you can
make changes easily.

CHAPTER 12

Making Parenting Work

This might seem overwhelming to you. Parenting is not easy. But, just to give my personal testimony, the joy of seeing your child grow into maturity, into a well-grounded individual who is living out their God-given purpose...well, there's just absolutely nothing that can substitute for that. Once you begin this journey, you will find yourself thinking of even more creative ways to successfully shepherd your child through this thing we call life.

These are seeds we're planting here. The work you put in on the front end will pay off in amazing ways on the back end!

It's time to get started. And you're not alone. The resources in these next sections and in the Appendices provide additional resources and tips.

Blessings on your journey!

To book Yvonne Posey Gilchrist as a guest speaker, please feel free to email her at:

yvonne@positioningyourchild.com

APPENDIX I

College Preparation Checklist for Students

Taken from
http://www.eduers.com/sat/college_preparation.htm

Pre-High School –

- Take challenging classes in English, mathematics, science, history, geography, the arts, and a foreign language.

- Develop strong study skills.

- Start thinking about which high school classes will best prepare you for college.

- If you have an opportunity to choose among high schools, or among different programs within one high school, investigate the options and determine which ones will help you further your academic and career interests and open doors to many future options.

- Investigate different ways to save money - buying a U.S. Savings Bond or opening a savings account in a bank, investing in mutual funds, etc.

- Start saving for college if you haven't already.

High School:

9th Grade -

- Take challenging classes in English, mathematics, science, history, geography, a foreign language, government, civics, economics, and the arts.
- Get to know your career counselor or guidance counselor, and other college resources available in your school.
- Talk to adults in a variety of professions to determine what they like and dislike about their jobs and what kind of education is needed for each kind of job.
- Continue to save for college.

10th Grade –

- Take challenging classes in English, mathematics, science, history, geography, a foreign language, government, civics, economics, and the arts.
- Talk to adults in a variety of professions to determine what they like and dislike about their jobs, and what kind of education is needed for each kind of job.

- Become involved in school- or community-based extracurricular (before or after school) activities that interest you and/or enable you to explore career interests.

- Meet with your career counselor or guidance counselor to discuss colleges and their requirements.

- Take the Preliminary Scholastic Assessment Test/National Merit Scholarship Qualifying Test (PSAT/NMSQT). You must register early. If you have difficulty paying the registration fee, see your guidance counselor about getting a fee waiver.

- Take advantage of opportunities to visit colleges and talk to students.

- Continue to save for college.

11th Grade

- Take challenging classes in English, mathematics, science, history, geography, a foreign language, government, civics, economics, and the arts.

- Meet with your career counselor or guidance counselor to discuss colleges and their requirements.

- Continue involvement in school- or community-based extracurricular activities.

- Decide which colleges most interest you. Write these schools to request information and an application for admission. Be sure to ask about special admissions requirements, financial aid, and deadlines.

- Talk to college representatives at college fairs.

- Take advantage of opportunities to visit colleges and talk to students.

- Consider people to ask for recommendations - teachers, counselors, employers, etc.

- Investigate the availability of financial aid from Federal, State, local, and private sources. Call the Student Aid Hotline at the U.S. Department of Education (1-800-4FED-AID) for a student guide to Federal financial aid. Talk to your guidance counselor for more information.

- Find out more about the domestic Peace Corps, called AmeriCorps, by calling 1-800-942-2677 or TDD 1-800-833-3722.

- Investigate the availability of scholarships provided by organizations such as corporations, labor unions, professional associations, religious organizations, and credit unions.

- If applicable, go to the library and look for directories of scholarships for women, minorities, and disabled students.

- Register for and take the Scholastic Assessment Test (SAT I), the ACT, SAT II Subject Tests, or any other exams required for admission to the colleges you might want to attend. If you have difficulty paying the registration fee, see your guidance counselor about getting a fee waiver.

- Continue to save for college.

12th Grade

- Take challenging classes in English, mathematics, science, history, geography, a foreign language, government, civics, economics, the arts, and advanced technologies.

- Meet with your counselor early in the year to discuss your plans.

- Complete all necessary financial aid forms. Make sure that you fill out at least one form that can be used for Federal aid.

Financial Preparation Checklist for Parents

Pre-High School –

- Investigate different ways to save money - buying U.S. Savings Bonds or opening a savings account in a bank, etc.

- Start saving money for your child's college education.

High School:

9th Grade

- Continue to save for college.

10th Grade

- Continue to save for college.

11th Grade

- Help your child investigate the availability of financial aid from Federal, State, local, and private sources. Call the Student Aid Hotline at the U.S. Department of Education (1-800-4FED-AID) for a student guide to Federal financial aid. Have your child talk to his or her guidance counselor for more information.

- Help your child investigate the availability of scholarships provided by organizations such as corporations, labor unions, professional associations, religious organizations, and credit unions.

- If applicable, go to the library with your son or daughter and look for directories on scholarships for women, minorities, and disabled students.

12th Grade

- Make sure your child completes all necessary financial aid forms. Be sure that he or she completes at least one form that can be used for Federal aid.

- Continue to save for college.

APPENDIX II

Narrowing the Field: Choosing Which College to Attend

By Alex Flagg, Educational Services Development Specialist, Working Solutions.

Now that you've been accepted into your colleges of choice, you may face a special dilemma - you can only go to one! How do you decide between all these schools when you want to go to them all? Follow these tips to help you make the best decision about your future.

Visit the Schools –

Perhaps the most important thing you can do when making the final decision about your college career is to visit the school personally. Even though making visits to your prospective colleges can be expensive, it is much cheaper than attending for a few years, realizing you don't like it and having to transfer elsewhere.

Most schools run open houses or admitted student days to allow prospective students a chance to get a feel for the school. During these events, you will most likely stay with a student who attends the school or works with the admissions office; if you have this option, take it. You can get a much better idea of student life from the people who live it than from an admissions counselor.

Community Considerations –

The culture of the college may be the most important thing you need to assess on your visit. Too many students ignore the importance of community when looking at a school, instead considering the 'name' and reputation of the college. Always remember that when you visit a school, you are not just going to be attending school there; you will be living there.

- Get a feel for the dorm atmosphere: are the dorms split between classes, into special interests, or only used by first year students?
- What is the social scene like? What organizations host parties? What role do Greek organizations play in social life? Is the school a 'party' school or is it fairly quiet? What are the major student holidays or social events sponsored by the college (such as a spring day, barn dances, concerts, retreats, trips, etc.)?
- What activities do students enjoy? What clubs, intramural sports and extracurricular activities are popular? Where do students hang out on campus and in town?

- What is the college's physical environment? Do you like the climate, the campus and the buildings? Is the college spread out over a huge area or packed tightly together? What services and facilities are available on the campus? Ask a few students what the weather is like during the summers and winters to get a better idea of what you can expect over the course of the year.

- Go to the cafeteria and food service facilities. Is the food good or bad? Do they offer a variety of cuisine (such as vegetarian, kosher, multiple main courses) or just one offering at each meal? Is the cafeteria a meeting place for students to hang out?

- Check out safety and security issues. Is the campus "dry" or does it have an open alcohol policy? What are the policies on drugs? What hours is the student health center open for use? Does the campus have a good security team? Is the campus well lit?

- Off campus life is just as important as on-campus life. What is the town surrounding the campus like? What is there to do nearby? How close is the campus to off-campus goods and services? How does the college relate to the town (i.e. is it a 'college' town or not?). Is off-campus housing available?

- How do students get around? Is public transportation or transportation through the school available?

Educational Considerations -

The reason you and your family are shelling out tens of thousands of dollars is for you to get a good education. Use this list as you consider the following factors:

- Before you register for a visit, sit down and make a list of the courses and majors you are interested in or good at. Keep the list broad – leave room for you to explore new facets of your education and learn new things about yourself in school. Oftentimes, students discover disciplines they never had known about in high school and many students who enter a school as one major end up graduating with a diploma in something totally different.

- Look at a list of course offerings for the current semester. How many classes are there you would be interested in taking? Are all the subjects you are interested in offered at this school?

- When you visit, attend a day of classes if possible. What was the class size? How did the professor communicate with the students – was it large and impersonal or small and intimate? Were the students engaged in the discussion with the instructor? You can get a good idea of a school's culture by attending just a few courses.

- Talk to students and faculty. What are the strongest departments and majors in the school? Are there any programs with extensive funding, off-campus education opportunities or special facilities? What are the weakest or smallest departments?

- What facilities does the college offer to students free of charge (i.e. computer lab, email and internet services, library, sports center, etc)? What is the quality of these facilities?

- What is the reputation of the school? Is it known where you grew up or where you plan to live? Remember, a reputation does not mean you will get the best education for your learning style and circumstances. You will take away what you put into college – if a college engages you, challenges you and has an environment you can thrive in, it doesn't matter how well-known it is.

Personal and Family Considerations -

Everyone grows up in the college years – you leave the nest, striking out to live on your own and discover the world on your own terms. But that doesn't mean you won't want or need to go back home. Making some good decisions about distance, travel and your readiness to be "on your own" now can save you many problems later.

- Consider the actual distance of the school from home. How do you feel about being this far away? What are you going to miss because of the distance – birthdays, weddings, anniversaries, holidays or other special gatherings?

- How expensive is it to travel home? How long does it take? Some places can be further away, but much easier/cheaper to travel to (for instance being at a large city 1500 miles away rather than a small town 12 hours away by car).

- Finally, are you ready to be this far away from home? How strong are your ties to your parents, siblings, pets, friends and other relatives – how often do you need to see them? Really consider this carefully, because if you do travel too far from home, there is little remedy but to transfer to a closer school.

Financial Considerations -

Finally, you need to consider your financial situation. College is often the first major financial responsibility that you will take on – how you handle it will have significant effect on your credit rating and financial future as a young adult. Think these questions over carefully before making any commitments:

- Examine your costs. There are quite a few 'hidden' costs that you may not think about when planning financially for school. Expect to pay for food, books, living expenses, entertainment and extracurricular activities in addition to tuition and housing. How do these factors change your economic outlook?

- What will your loans look like? Too many students see their loans as free money, but common loans like the Federal Application for Student Aid (FAFSA) have their repayment period stretched over 10 years. That is a long time to be shelling out four- or five-hundred dollars a month for a few years of college bliss.

- Can you really afford to go here? What is the cost in out-of-pocket payments? In loans? How many grants have you received in your initial package?

- If money is an issue for you, what are other, less expensive acceptable alternatives? Have you been accepted to another less-expensive school that offers approximately the same variety of classes or programs as your first choice? How significant are the differences to you? Would attending a two-year or community college help your financial situation?

- What can you do to ease economic burdens – work/study jobs, internships, grants or scholarships? What is the tradeoff in terms of school time and social time? How big a difference would working make on your loans and payments?

- Are there other sources of money available to you? By the time you are accepted to colleges, it is usually too late to apply for federal or state aid, but colleges have specific grants and scholarships for new and returning students. Talk with a student recruiter or the admissions office to find out more about your options.

- Is there anyone you can talk with to revise your package? If you need to go to your first choice – or if it is your only viable alternative – are there any other factors on your application that could be revised or reviewed? Call your recruiter and set an appointment to go over your package step-by-step to see what you can do to get a better financial aid package.

Conclusion –

College is an experience that transcends learning from books – it is the beginning of your journey as an independent adult. Making your final decision on which college to attend is never easy; there are so many factors it can be overwhelming. Always remember, the decisions you make about college are never final until you walk away with a diploma – you always have the option of going to a school that better fits your needs, a major that piques your interest or exploring new facets of yourself. But good decisions now can save you a lot of grief in terms of your financial, educational, social and personal life.

APPENDIX III

Writing an Effective College Essay

By Alex Flagg, Educational Services Development Specialist, Working Solutions.

The college application is the first step into your new life as an adult. College will help you learn who you are, what you want out of life and how to make it on your own. But like all first steps, making the right choices with your college essay can be difficult. Make wise decisions about your essay and there is no telling where life's journey will take you.

Planning –

A large part of your time should be spent planning for your essay. You should start reflecting on your topic before you write a word. Try these questions to get yourself thinking in the right direction:

- What are your major accomplishments, both personal and academic? Why are they accomplishments?

- What views, attributes or skills do you have that are unique?
- What are you passions? What inspires you or keeps you centered?
- Do you have a strong belief – such as a philosophy, faith or set of principals – that you live by?
- What is your favorite art, book, film, etc.
- What was the most difficult time in your life and why?
- Have you ever overcome a great challenge? Why and how did you succeed?
- Have you ever faced a great challenge and failed? What did you learn?
- What would you like to be doing right now? Who would you want to be with? Where would you like to be? Why do you love these things so?
- Have you ever had an epiphany, something that revealed a great truth to you? What was it and when?
- What is your strongest personality trait? Why do you think so?
- What have you done outside of the classroom, as an individual or citizen of the world?
- What are your dreams for the future? What do you want to do with the education you will be getting at this college? What do you need to do to feel successful?

If you are stuck, you still have resources to get your thinking in the right direction. Try getting help from people close to you such as family, friends, fellow students or co-workers – they can provide new perspectives on what makes you unique. You can also look at other people's work; it is always good to be familiar with the competition. If you can, get a hold of an earlier essay that was turned into the school you are applying to. If you don't have access to one, take a look at other people's applications to the schools they went to.

Choosing Your Topic –

Once you have reflected on your topic, it is time to start the real work. Your topic is the heart of your essay, so it needs to be really strong. With your favorite list of topics in hand, put them under the lens of these criticisms to choose the best one for your essay:

- Do you have one really strong idea chosen for your topic?
- Is your topic personal? Is it manageable in the context of 1-2 pages? If not, you may want to consider making it smaller – the best topics are personal, contained and original. The more unique to you it is, the better.
- How passionate are you about your topic? This passion can translate into a better essay than something you are not enthused or inspired by.

- Does your topic discuss something of importance to you that you can use vivid personal experiences to describe? Can you frame those examples in fully realized paragraphs?
- Can you fully answer the question asked with your topic? Can you do so within any word or page limits? Can you address the topic competertly with quality answers and factual information? If you cannot answer the question, keep to the proper size or prove that you know and understand your subject, it is best to choose another. No one appreciates a faker.
- Is your topic interesting? Grabbing the reader's attention is critical, as most likely the reviewer will only spend a few minutes reading your work – so make them count.
- Is your topic broad enough to answer multiple questions? Using a topic you know well enough that you can answer multiple questions will save you time and effort.
- Does your topic fit your application? How does it meet the character of the school you are applying for?
- Does the essay fill in the blank spots of your application? You can use the essay to explain inconsistencies – if you have a 1450 SAT score but only a 2.0 GPA, you can explain the contradiction. Be careful not to turn your essay into an excuse; keep your explanations concise and convincing.

Writing –

Writing the essay is actually the easiest part of the process, if you have planned well. Most of the tricks to writing an effective essay are common sense, but there are also special rules and expectations you should remain aware of. Review your topic and get writing with these pointers:

Answer the question –

If you don't answer the question asked by the college, your application will not be considered further.

Be original and keep it fresh –

Is there a better way to say something? Find the best possible way to express yourself and connect emotionally with the reader. For example, instead of saying "I had to get up early to make money for my new car," you could say "For two years I awoke at the crack of dawn and started working in the fields to save up for my first car."

Speak to their emotions –

The people reading your entrance essays are not English professors or judges who will penalize you for every mistake you make – chances are they are overworked admissions staff who have already read 50 essays before they get to yours. Reach out and touch their emotions, not with hokey morals or sappy stories, but with images that create an emotional impression. According to the Cambridge Essay Service, "the very best conclusion a reader can reach is, 'I really like this kid."

Give of yourself –

This essay is really about you – try to show the recruiter your writing ability as well as your personality, your interests, the experiences and the ideas that have made you the person you are. Be strategic – show the school the 'academic' you if you are counting on your strength as a student, or the 'adventurous' you if you are taking a big risk by moving far from home or to a really challenging school. Discuss issues that move you, thoughts you have lived by, experiences – but stay away from discussing the 'big issues' in general. There are a lot of people who can argue those points better – that's why you are going to college in the first place!

Show, don't tell –

This is one of the most basic lessons you will learn in a college English course – it is always better to show your reader what they need to see, rather than tell them. Just because you tell a college essay reviewer you are a smart person who deserves to attend their school doesn't mean they will believe you. You must convince them by showing evidence – be it through examples or anecdotes you have learned over the course of your life.

Use vivid imagery and prose –

Part of the 'show not tell' rule is to create examples that will ring in your reader's mind. Be specific when using examples so you can create the emotional impression you seek. Powerful or poignant images will help the reader grasp what you experienced and create empathy.

Big words don't make good essays –

Keep your language clear and elegant. Using big words will neither impress the admissions reviewer nor improve the quality of your essay – they are best used in appropriate situations.

Focus on your introduction -

First impressions mean a lot. You can expect an admission officer to read your essay for only 1-2 minutes, so it is critical you grab their interest with a solid introduction. The introduction should be structured in a way that it does not summarize your essay, but rather creates 'intrigue' to draw your reader into the piece. Starting your essay off with a question, a strong statement or a quote that reflects your topic without summarizing it are all good strategies for making your intro more successful. You can also rewrite your intro last, after you have written your essay – very often you may find a strong theme coming out in your piece as you wrote it that you did not see at first.

Tie the body and intro together –

At the same time, your intro must represent your body paragraphs accurately. A silly introduction will only serve to confuse the reader when they get into the piece – and create the impression that you are not serious about your essay, or getting into the school.

Make smooth transitions –

Good transitions help tie your essay together, show the logical flow of your piece and are the sign of a good writer. Transitions are more than just words and phrases such as "as a result", "in addition", "while..." and "since..." You can use other techniques such as repetition of key words and building your initial statement or title into each body paragraph to increase the overall quality of the piece.

Good conclusions -

The conclusion of a college application essay is a bit different from a standard high school essay. Since your topic is most likely short, there is no need to re-summarize your points. You should instead use the conclusion to expand on the broader implications of your discussion, frame your discussion in a larger context or show what you learned from your discussion. Try linking your conclusion to your introduction by reiterating key phrases or points to create a greater sense of balance. You should also try to end with a powerful thought, such as a famous quote that relates to your topic, to create a strong final impression.

Edit and revise –

After you take a break, have some people whom you trust and are analytical – parents, family friends, fellow students or teachers – read over and edit your essay. Get feedback from them on both the technical elements of the piece (consistency of voice, spelling, grammar, verbiage, etc.) and the quality (what are the best parts; what is memorable about it; is every sentence crucial to the whole; what does it say about you as a person; are there clichés; what needs more work). Spend as much time on your revisions as you can until you are satisfied with what you have. You left plenty of time to get the job done, right?

Don't go over the limit –

If you have a word limit, respect both the rules of the college and the reviewers and stay at or below that many words. This may be more work for you, but very often you can successfully eliminate parts of your work and make it even stronger.

Things to Avoid -

In the competitive world of college applications, many people will go to great lengths to get into their ideal school. However, there are certain rules colleges go by – spoken and unspoken – which you should be aware of before you turn in your final draft. Avoid these pitfalls:

Misrepresentation –

Everyone wants to get into their first-choice college; competition can be so tight at the best schools that every edge helps. However, it is only counterproductive to misrepresent yourself in your essay. Beyond being dishonest, lying or twisting the truth can cause you nothing but trouble; generally, the more competitive the school, the more closely they look at each fact in the application. Be straightforward about who you are and don't try to 'spruce up' your accomplishments if you can't back it up.

Gimmicks -

Making your topic seem "funny" or "silly" or "off the wall" ideas, topics or images used just to get attention can quickly backfire. It is very difficult to pull off and most admissions staff do not appreciate gimmicky approaches.

Repetition -

Are you just regurgitating information that is already covered by your application? If so, you may want to reconsider your topic. Find something new and fresh that can't be covered with a few lines or some numbers. Let them know *who* you are, not your statistics.

Overdone topics -

There are many popular themes reviewers see again and again in college application essays. If it is a popular topic, taking a new spin on it may be just the thing you need to stand out from the crowd. Try looking at CollegeGate.com's collection of sample essays (http://www.essayedge.com/) to get an idea of how students have approached their topics and how you can spruce those approaches up.

Controversy -

Is your topic controversial enough that it will turn off or tune out a large number of people? The goal of the college application essay is to create a positive impression – so the worst thing you can do is write an essay that is remembered negatively. Topics such as specific religions, political doctrines or controversial opinions are best left for after you get into the school of your choicc. If you have to tackle a controversial topic in your essay, be sure to handle in a way that is balanced and respectful of both sides of the issue. Show that you understand how others might not agree with you, but this is how the issue has influenced *your* life. Keeping the context personal will help you avoid offending others.

Pity -

If you are writing your essay based on how you survived difficult or traumatic experiences, be sure to focus on how they fit into the context of who you are. If you are not using the experience as a lens to magnify your personal characteristics, you are not writing a good essay. Just because something sad or hard happened to you doesn't mean you are a good candidate. College admissions staff know this. Nor do you want to be remembered as the pathetic student; rather, you should aspire to be remembered as the student who has developed impressive qualities under difficult circumstances.

Parading difference -

Some of the most pronounced differences between us, socially and physically, are differences in race, culture and sexual preference. When writing your essay it may be tempting to use difference as a starting point and an easy way to show you are a 'diverse' student. However, just as with life experiences, it is unwise to highlight this difference if it does not address the greater topic of who you are as a person. If you wish to address your minority status, do so in a way that shows you overcoming stigma, dealing with social ostracism and so forth. Admissions offers are not legally obligated – nor do they feel morally obligated – to admit a student based on a statistical, racial or cultural difference.

224

Your weak points -

Your essays goal is to make a good impression of a student ready for living independently, so avoid discussing your weak points when it isn't necessary. If the weakness is one that will affect your decision or ability to attend the school, such as being a recovering alcoholic who needs to be on a 'dry' campus, then you should consider mentioning it.

Conclusion -

One of the most difficult and confusing pieces of the college application process is the essay. This 200-500-word statement can be your key into the college of your dreams, if you do it well. Plan, write and scrutinize your piece; it may plant the seeds of a successful college education.